ARE YOU GONNA EAT THAT?

the essential collection of
they can talk comics

jimmy craig

Published by:
ULYSSES PRESS
PO Box 3440
Berkeley, CA 94703
www.ulyssespress.com

ISBN 978-1-64604-451-1
Library of Congress Catalog Number: 2022944060

Printed in China
2 4 6 8 10 9 7 5 3

Acquisitions editor: Casie Vogel
Managing editor: Claire Chun
Proofreader: Barbara Schultz
Production: Winnie Liu

To Nana,

for every comic strip you've cut out and mailed to me.

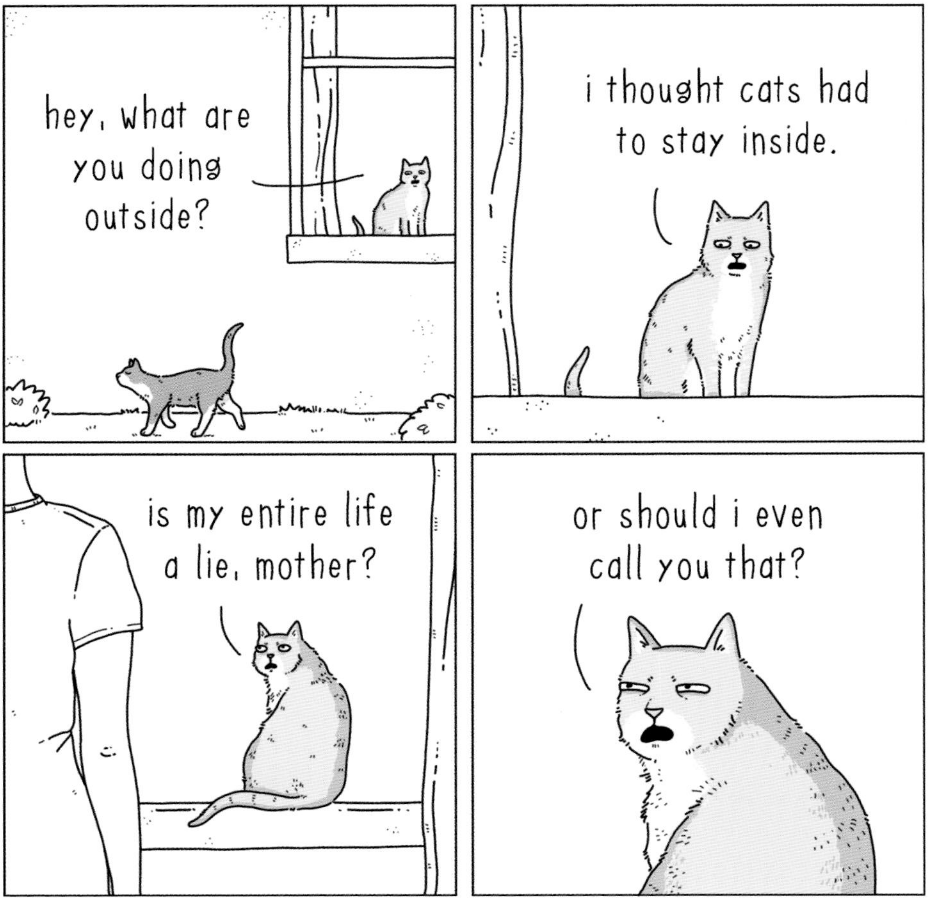
hey, what are you doing outside?
i thought cats had to stay inside.
is my entire life a lie, mother?
or should i even call you that?

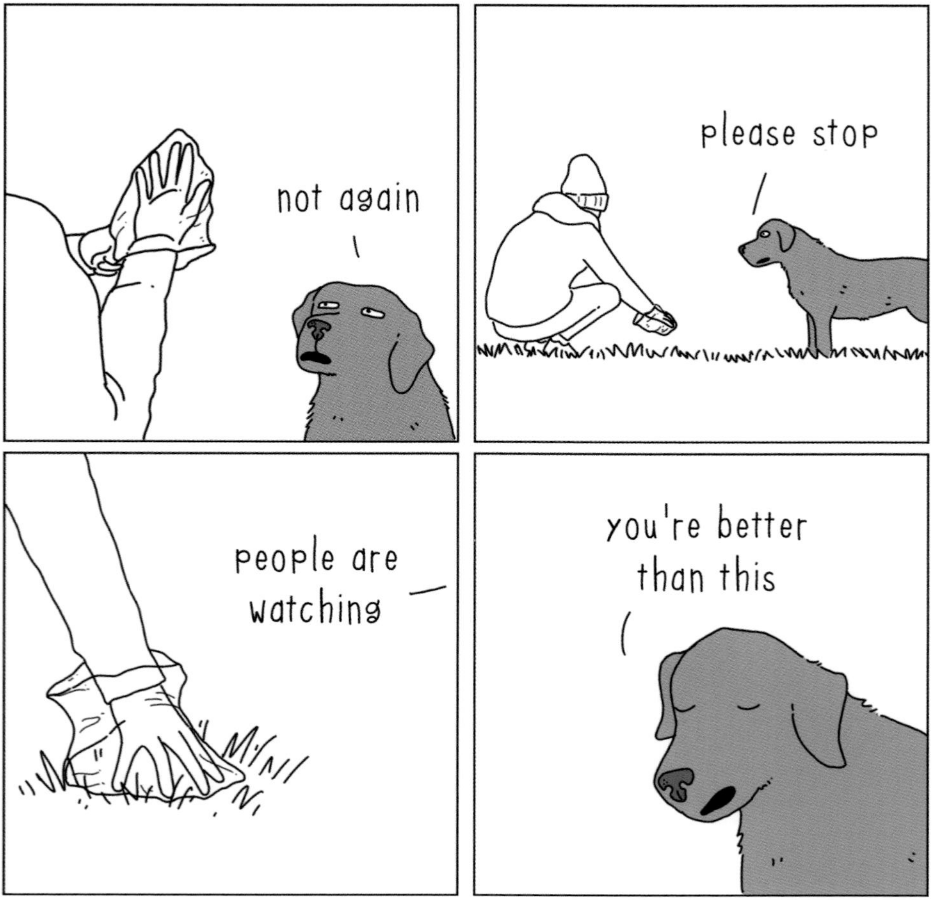
not again
please stop
people are watching
you're better than this

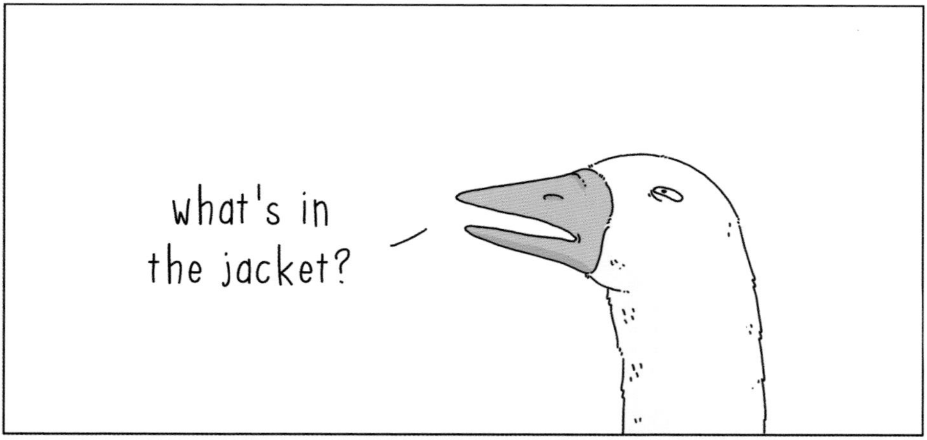
what's in
the jacket?

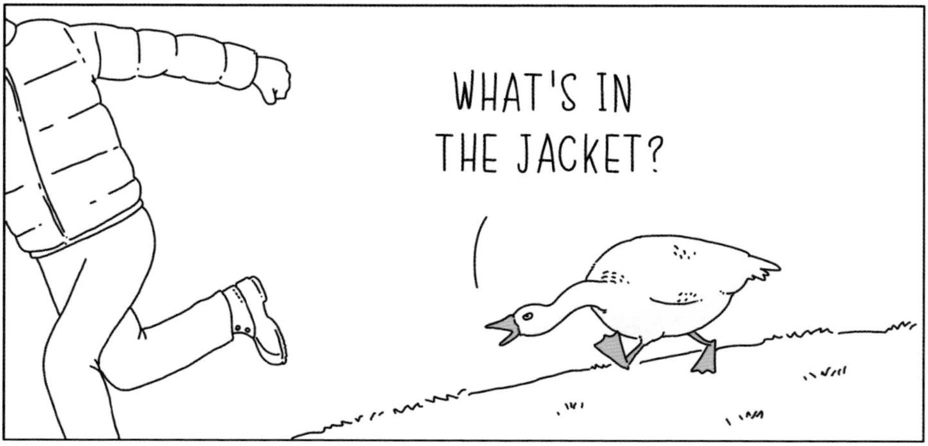
WHAT'S IN
THE JACKET?

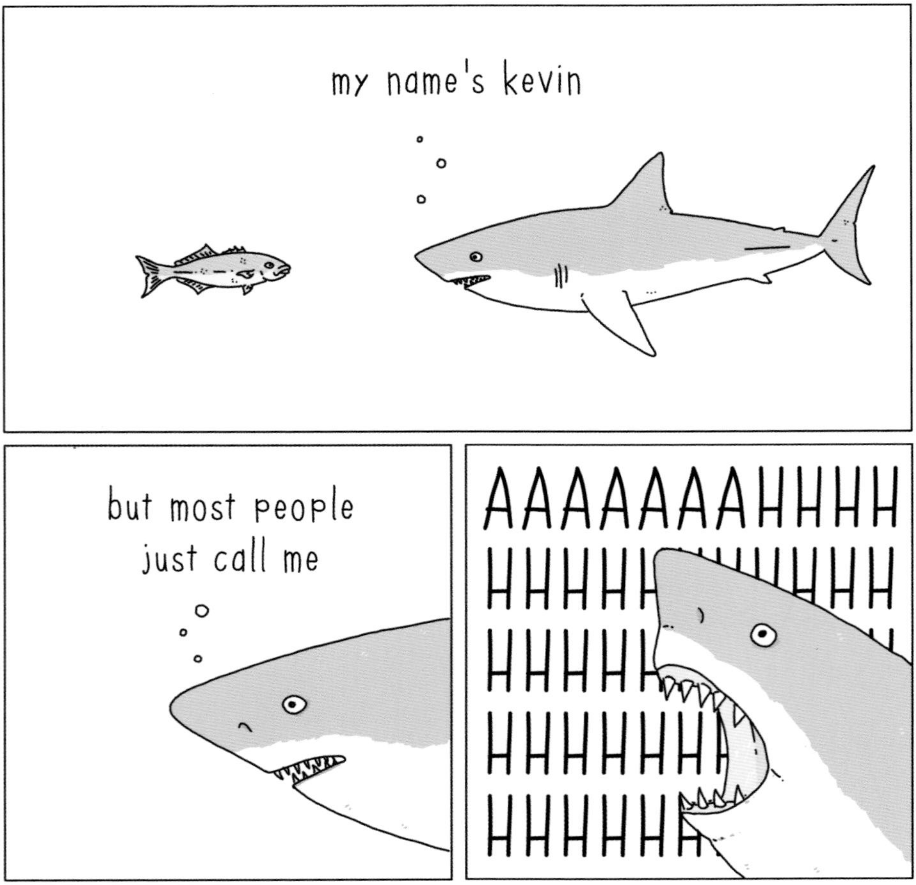
my name's kevin
but most people just call me
AAAAAAAHHHH

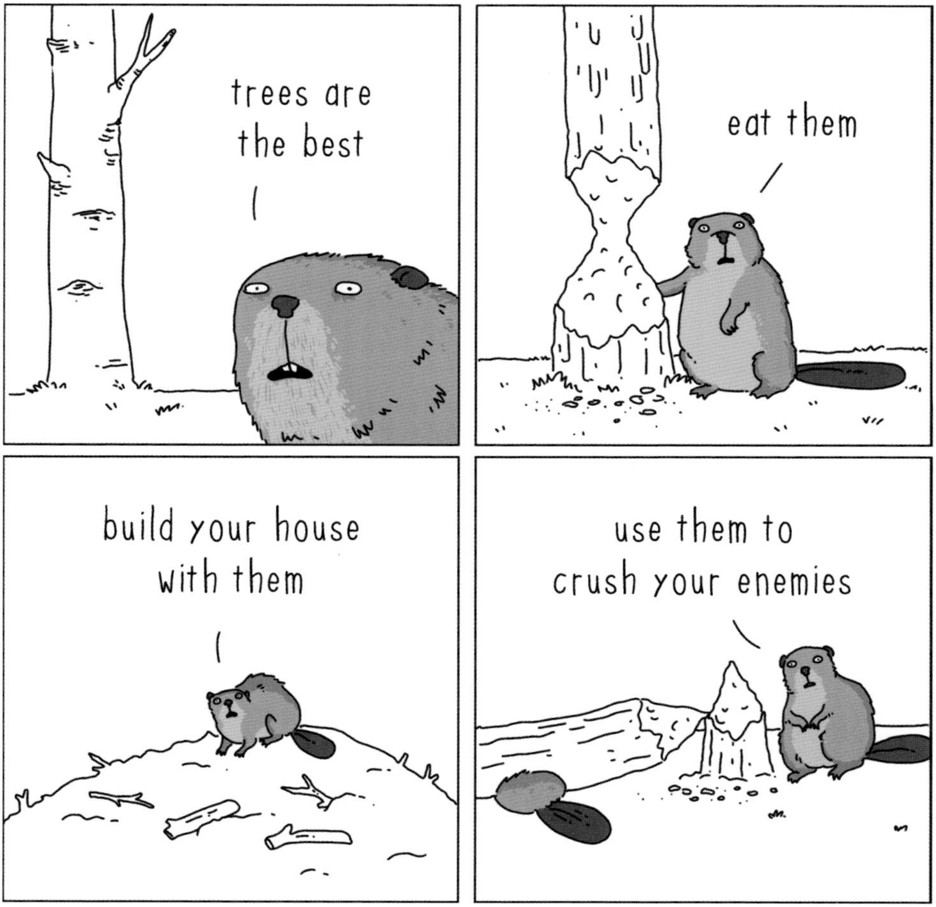
trees are
the best
eat them
build your house
with them
use them to
crush your enemies

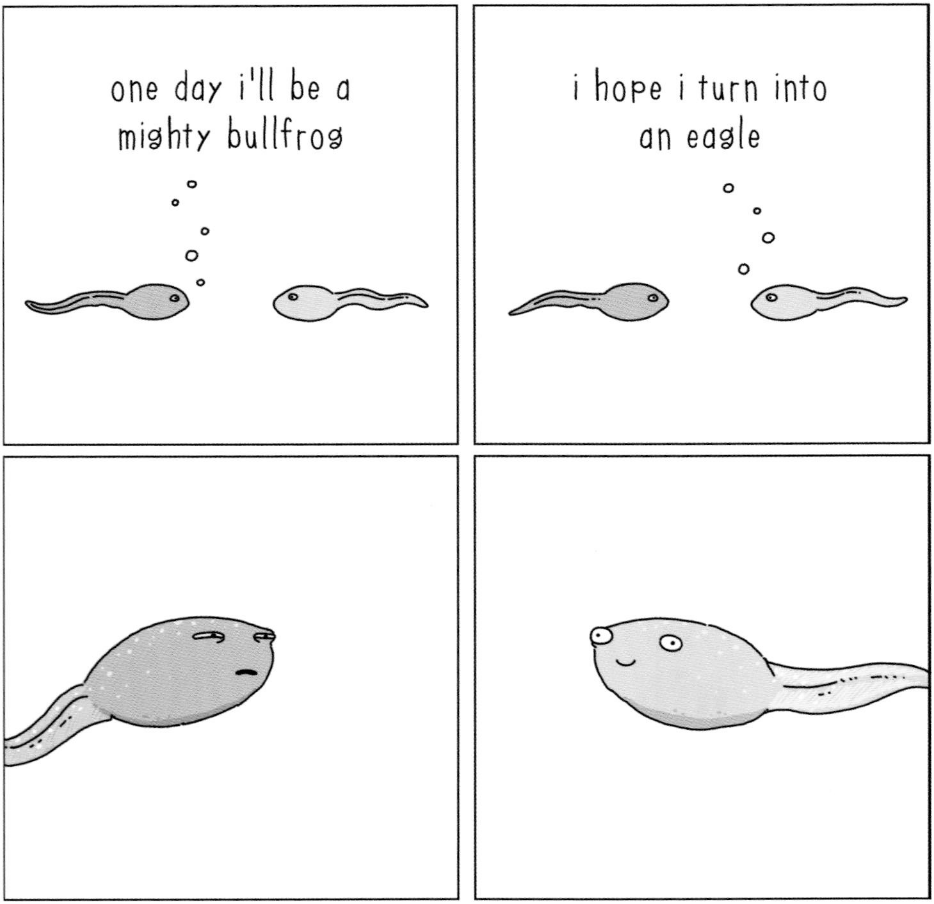
one day i'll be a mighty bullfrog
i hope i turn into an eagle

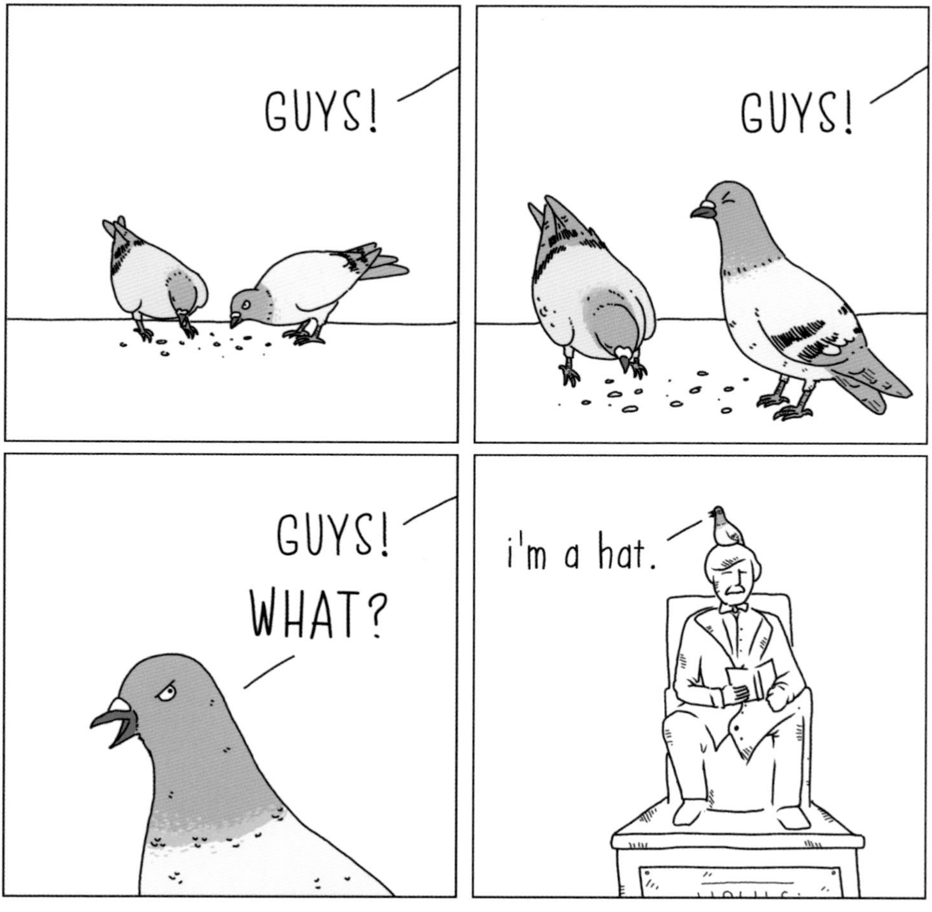
GUYS!
GUYS!
GUYS!
WHAT?
i'm a hat.

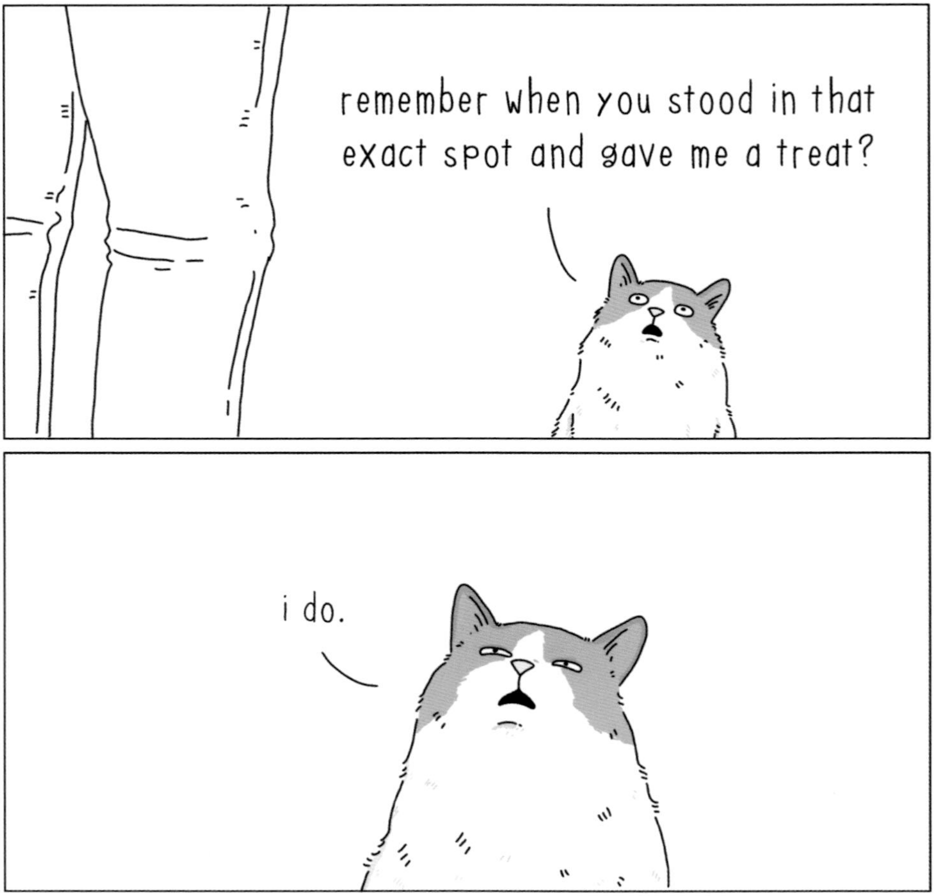
remember when you stood in that exact spot and gave me a treat?
i do.

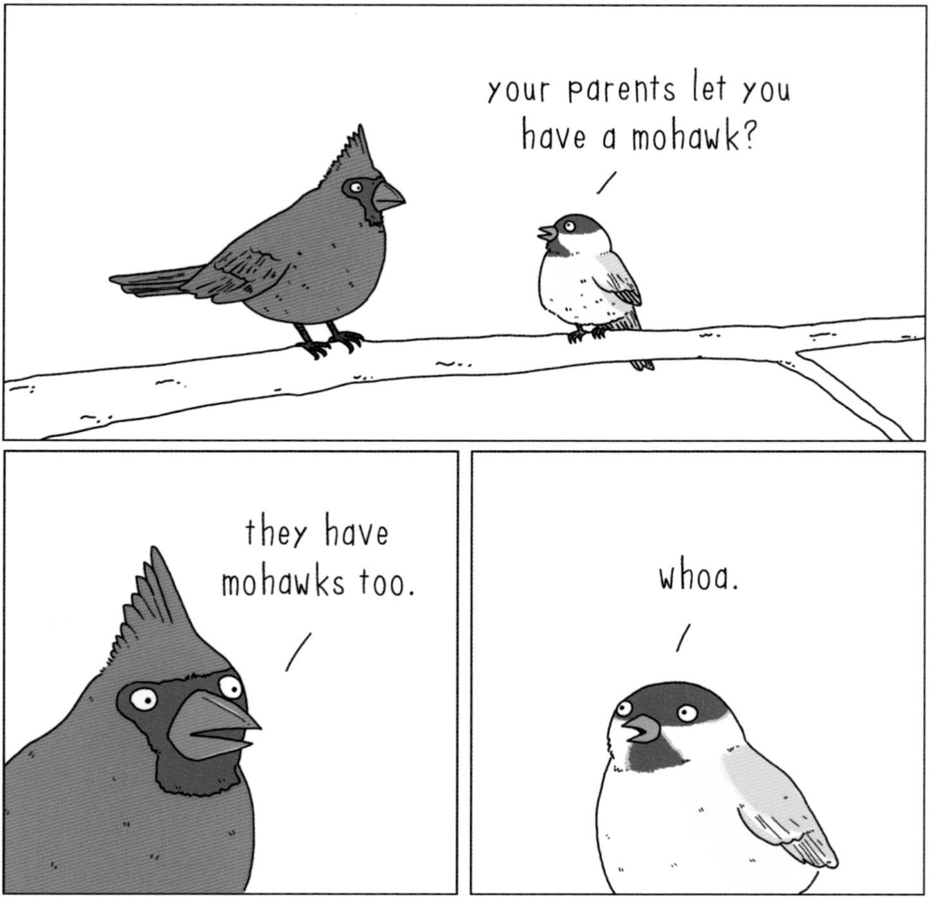
your parents let you have a mohawk?
they have mohawks too.
whoa.

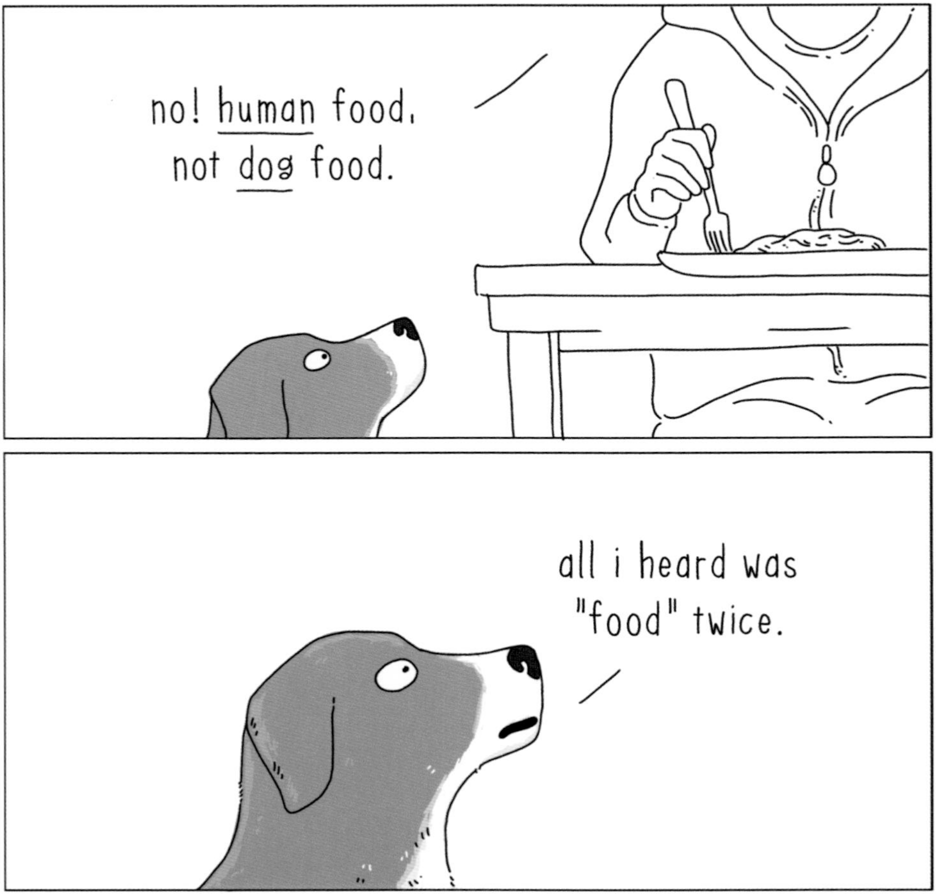
no! human food,
not dog food.
all i heard was
"food" twice.

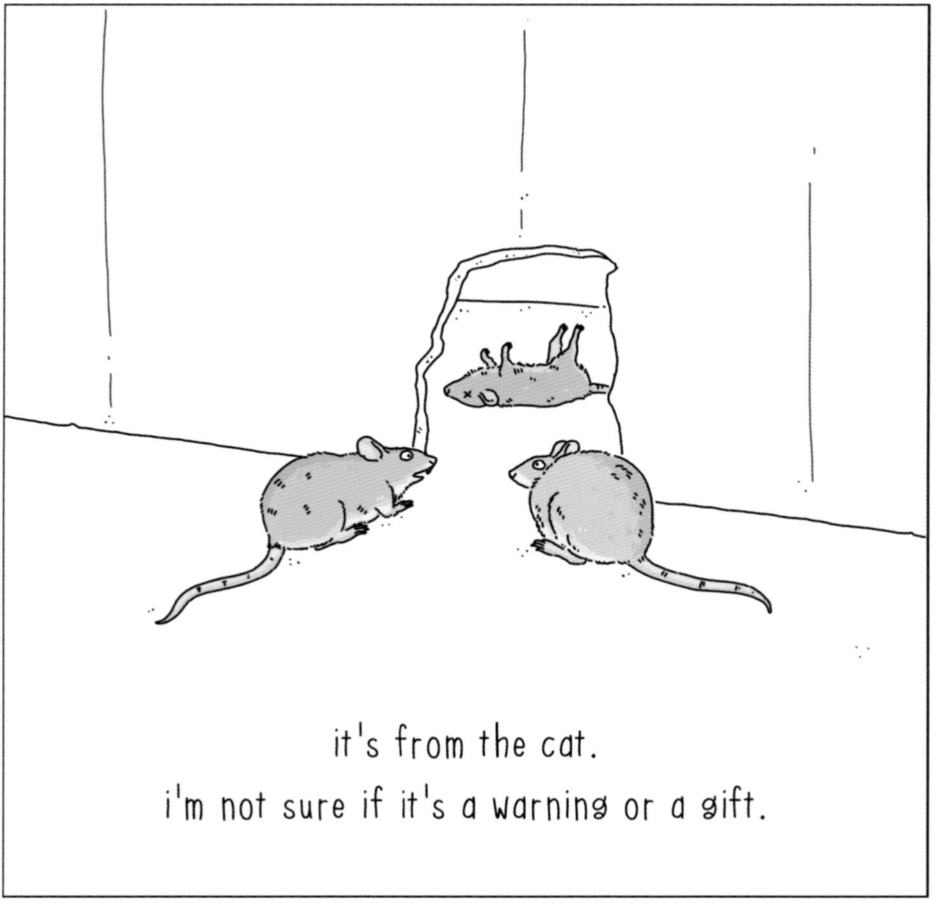

it's from the cat.
i'm not sure if it's a warning or a gift.

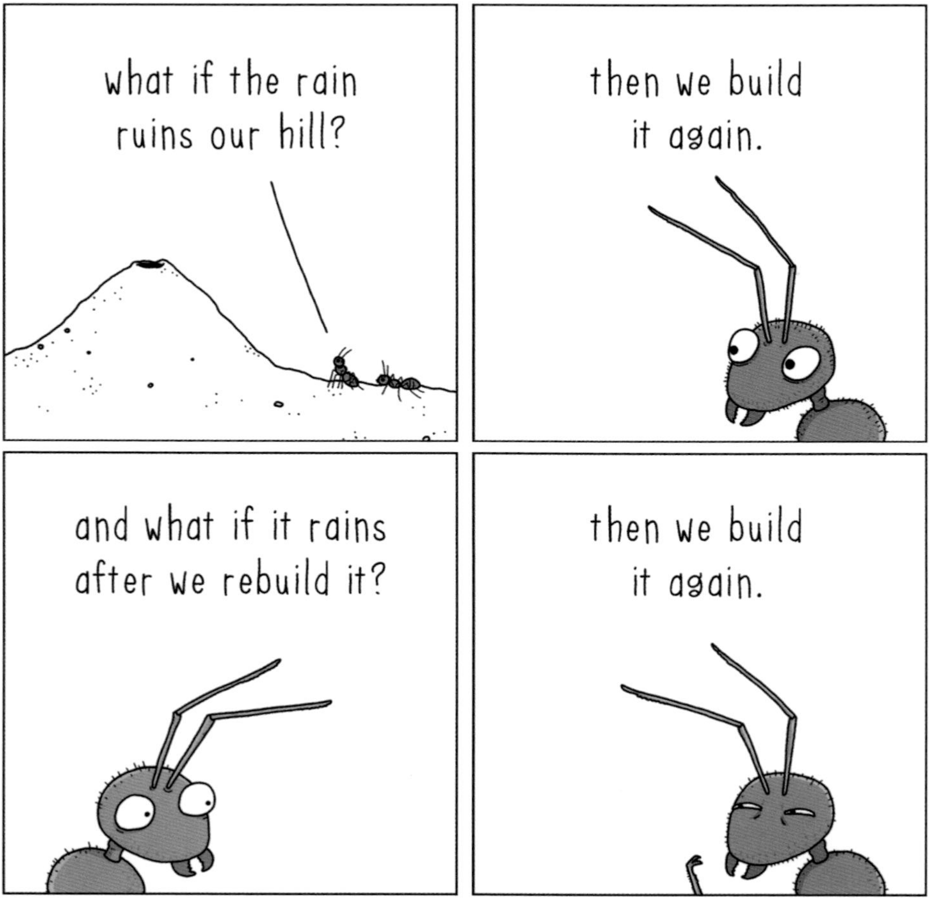
what if the rain ruins our hill?
then we build it again.
and what if it rains after we rebuild it?
then we build it again.

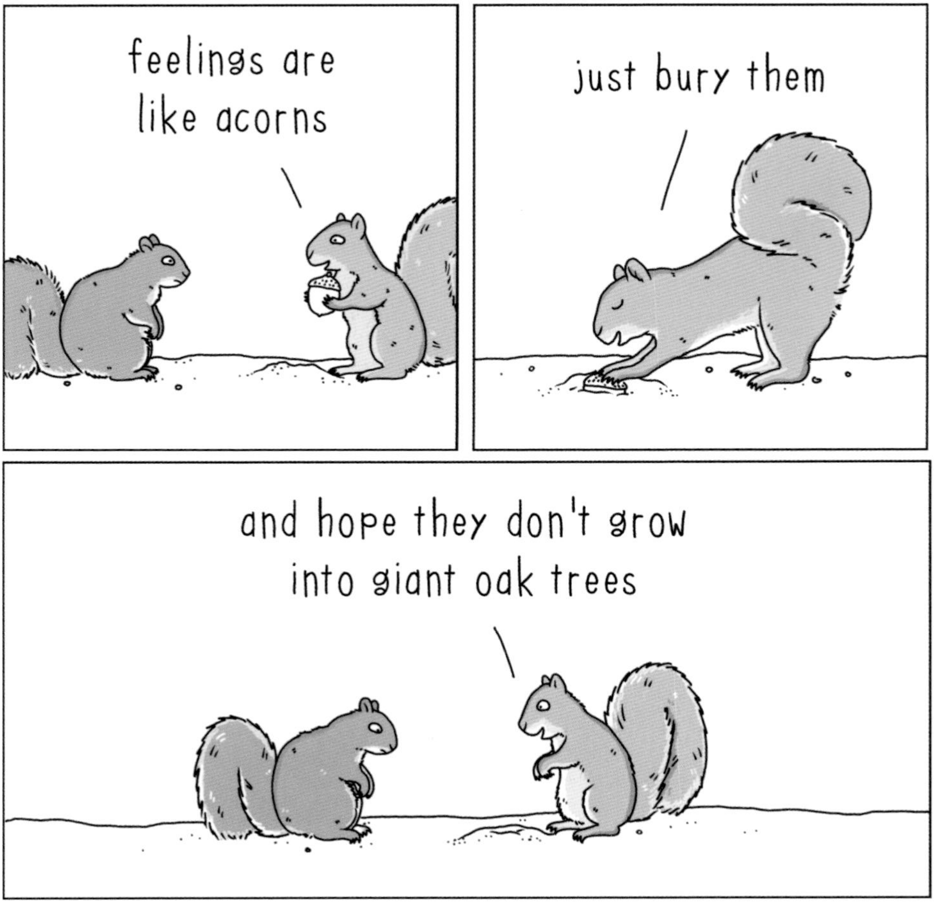
feelings are like acorns
just bury them
and hope they don't grow into giant oak trees

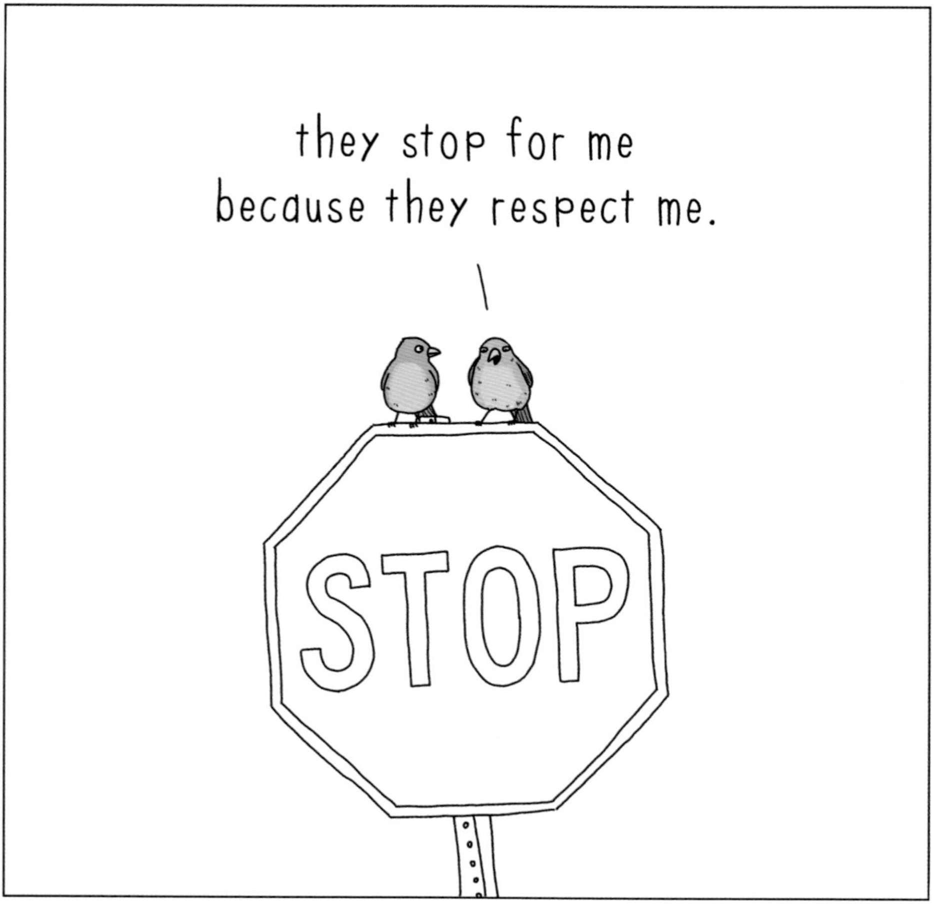
they stop for me
because they respect me.
STOP

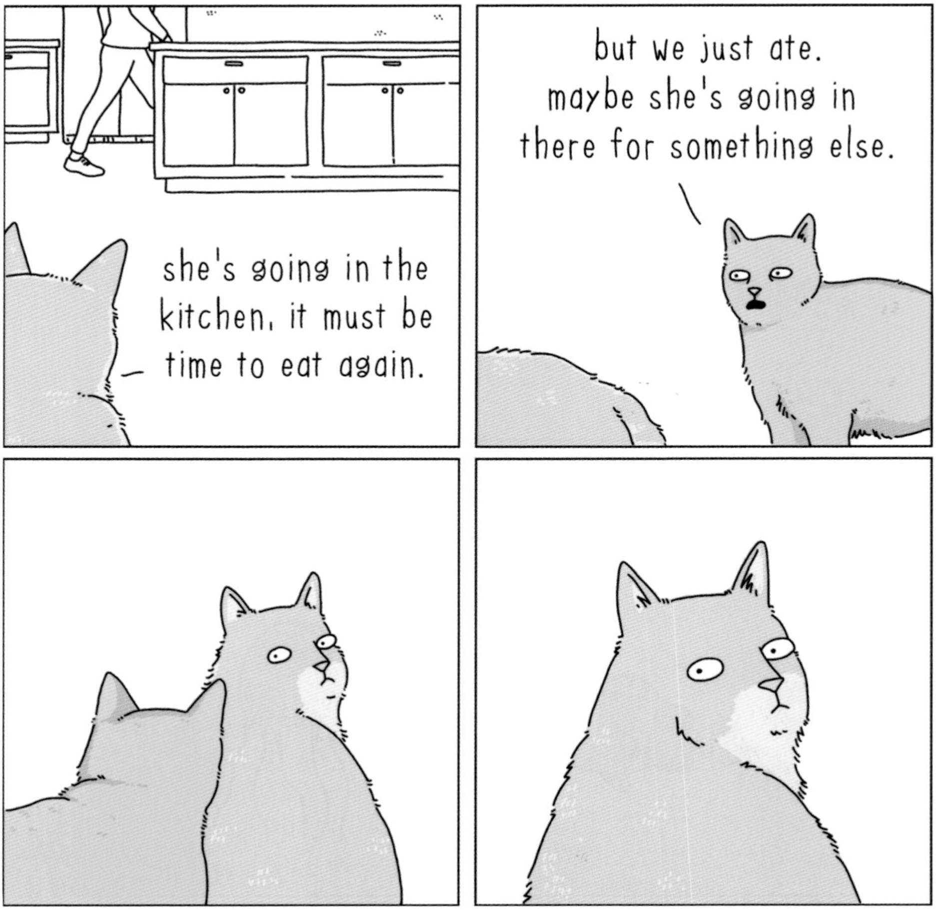
she's going in the kitchen, it must be time to eat again.
but we just ate. maybe she's going in there for something else.

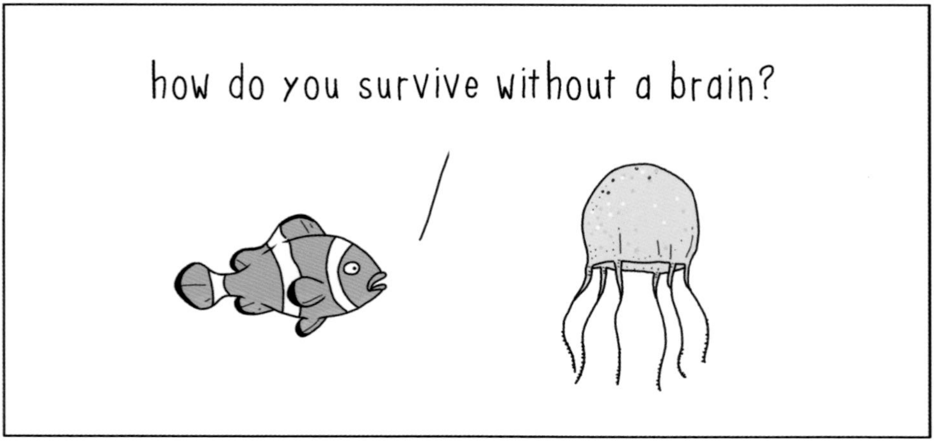
how do you survive without a brain?

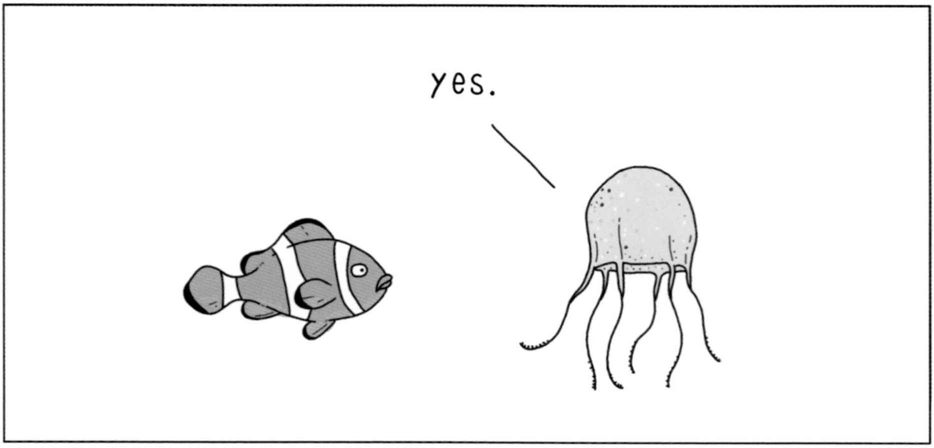
yes.

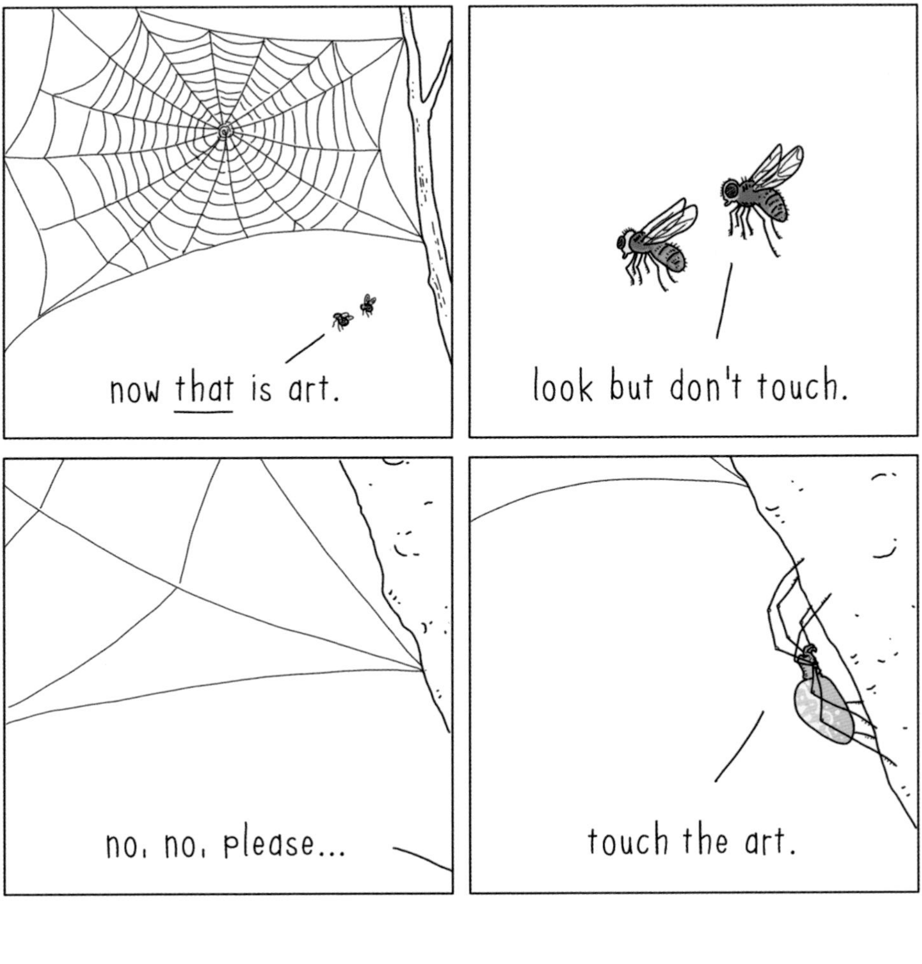
now that is art.
look but don't touch.
no, no, please...
touch the art.

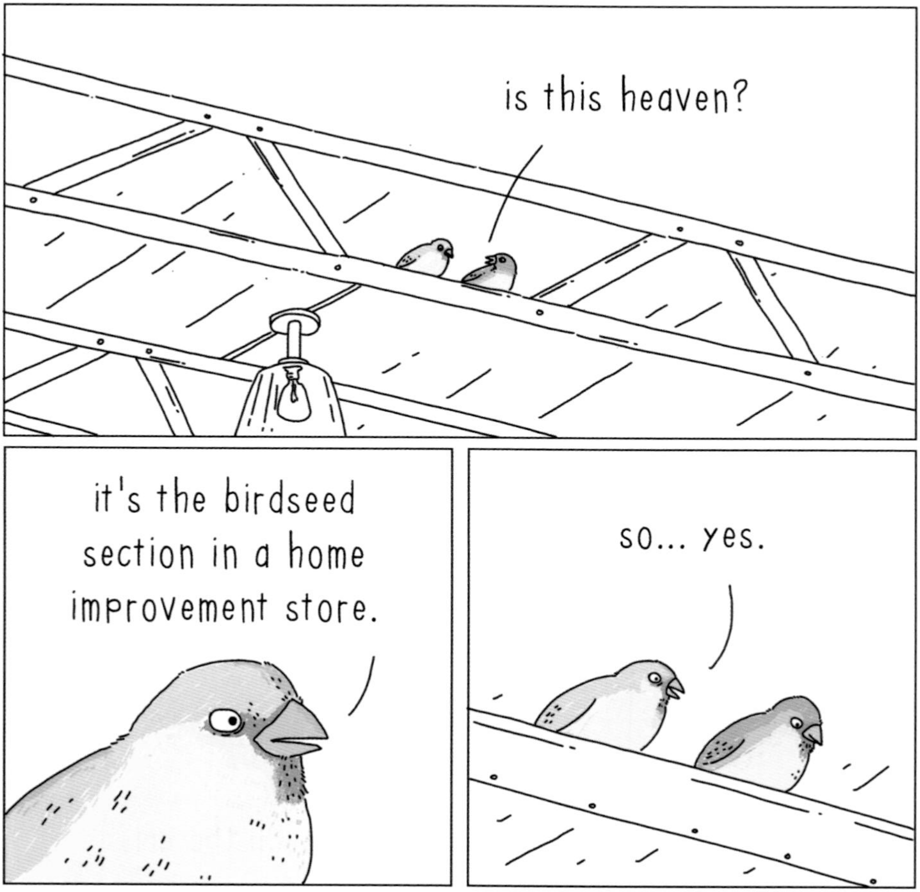
is this heaven?
it's the birdseed section in a home improvement store.
so... yes.

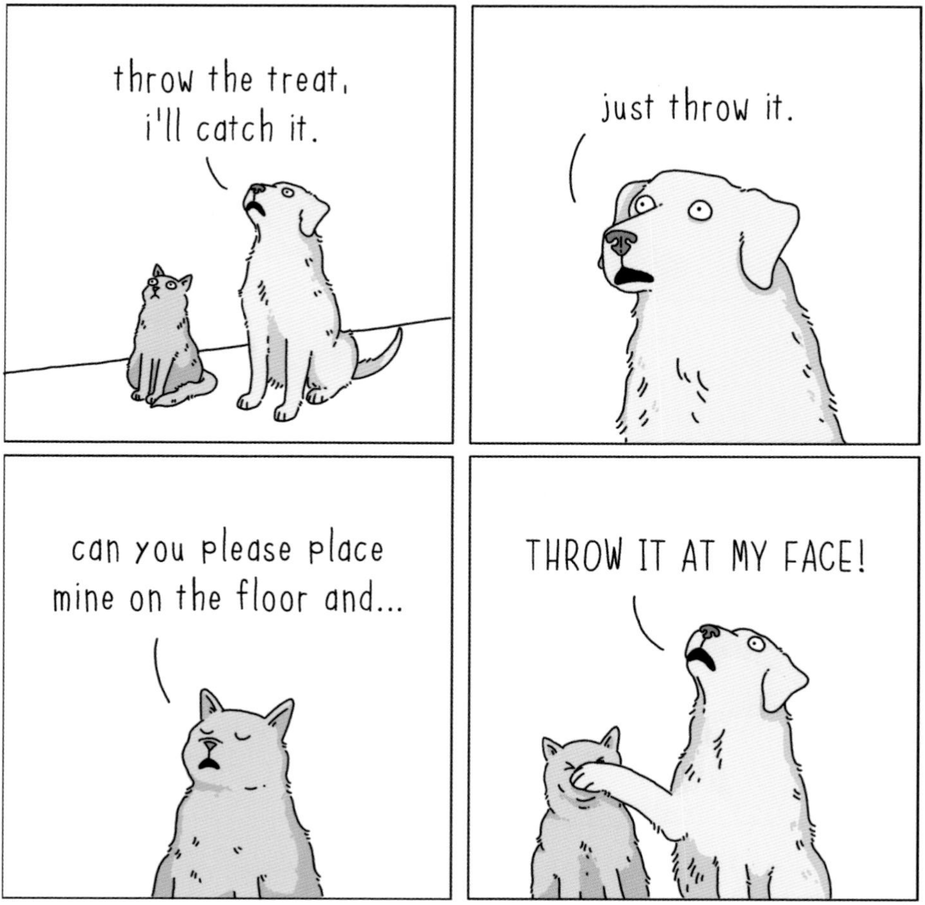
throw the treat, i'll catch it.
just throw it.
can you please place mine on the floor and...
THROW IT AT MY FACE!

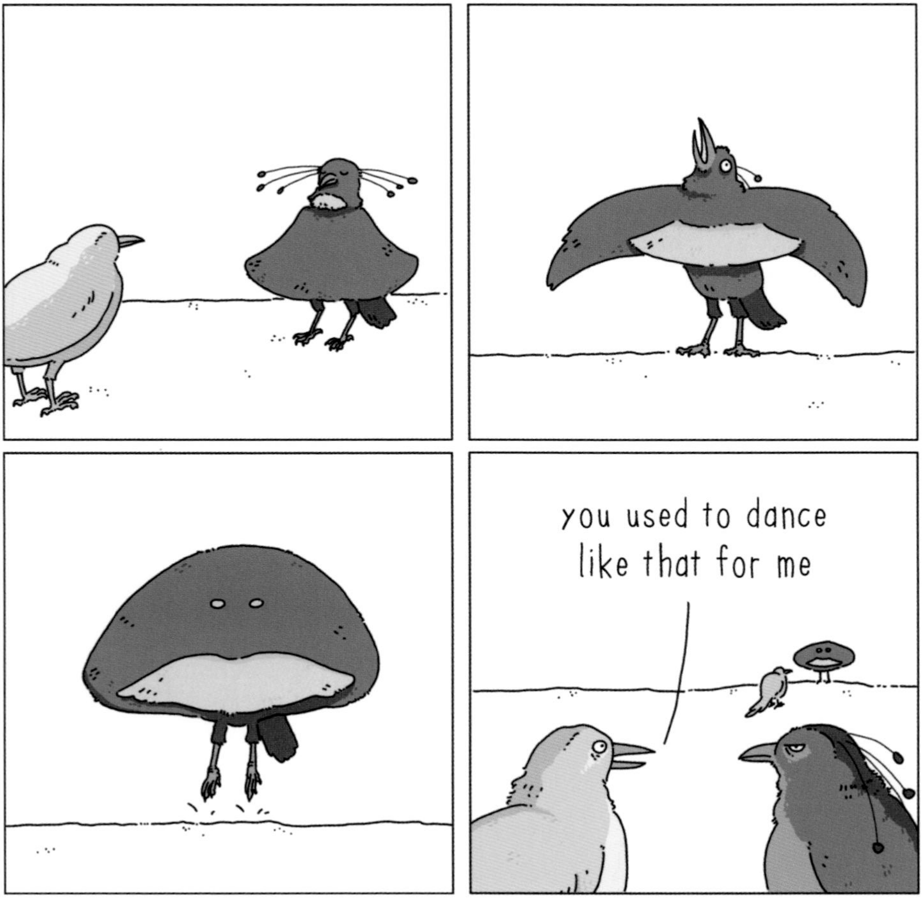
you used to dance
like that for me

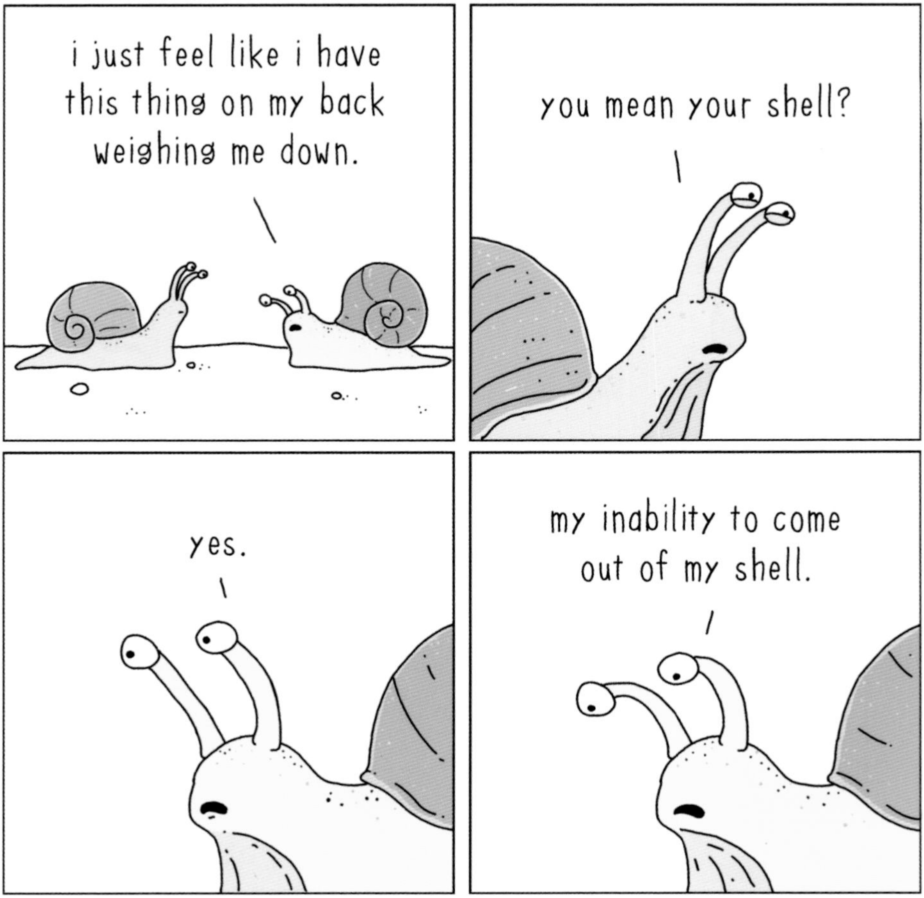
i just feel like i have this thing on my back weighing me down.
you mean your shell?
yes.
my inability to come out of my shell.

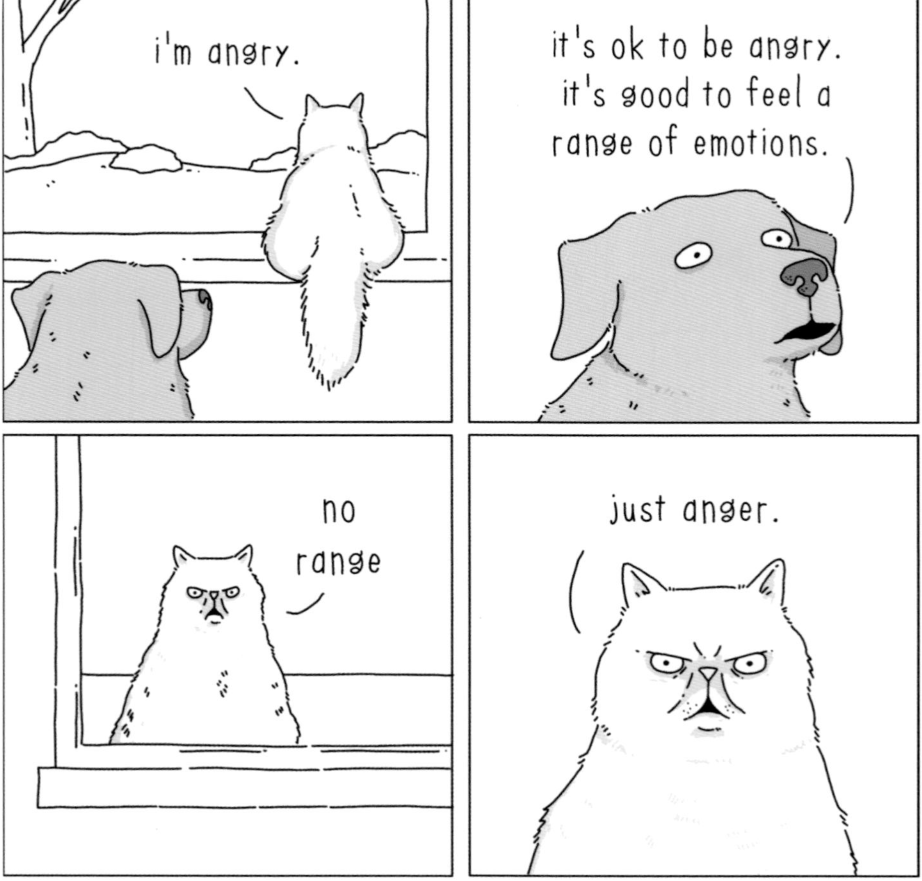
i'm angry.
it's ok to be angry. it's good to feel a range of emotions.
no range
just anger.

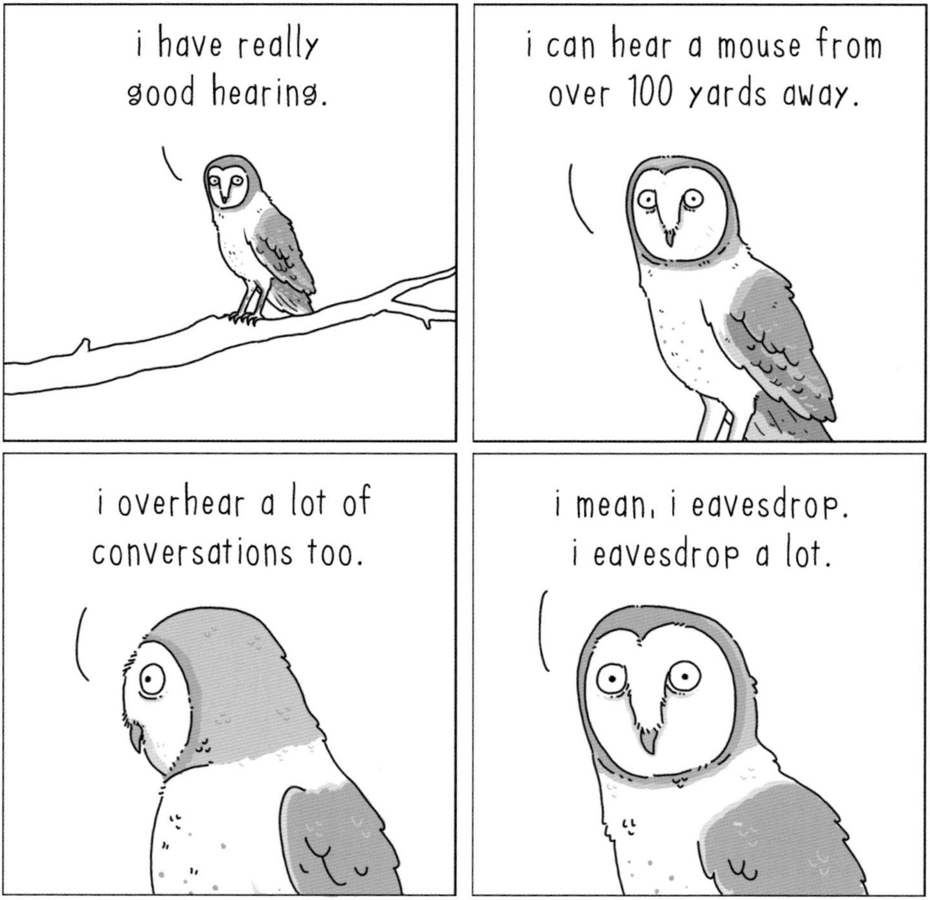
i have really
good hearing.
i can hear a mouse from
over 100 yards away.
i overhear a lot of
conversations too.
i mean, i eavesdrop.
i eavesdrop a lot.

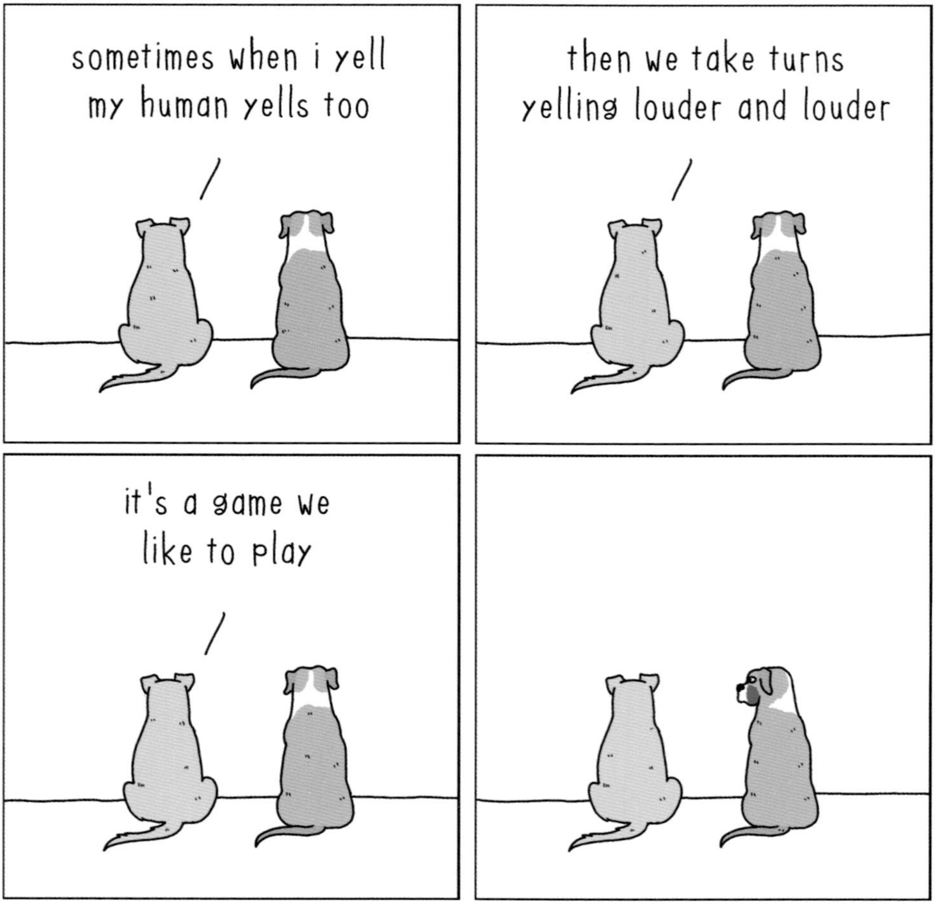
sometimes when i yell
my human yells too
then we take turns
yelling louder and louder
it's a game we
like to play

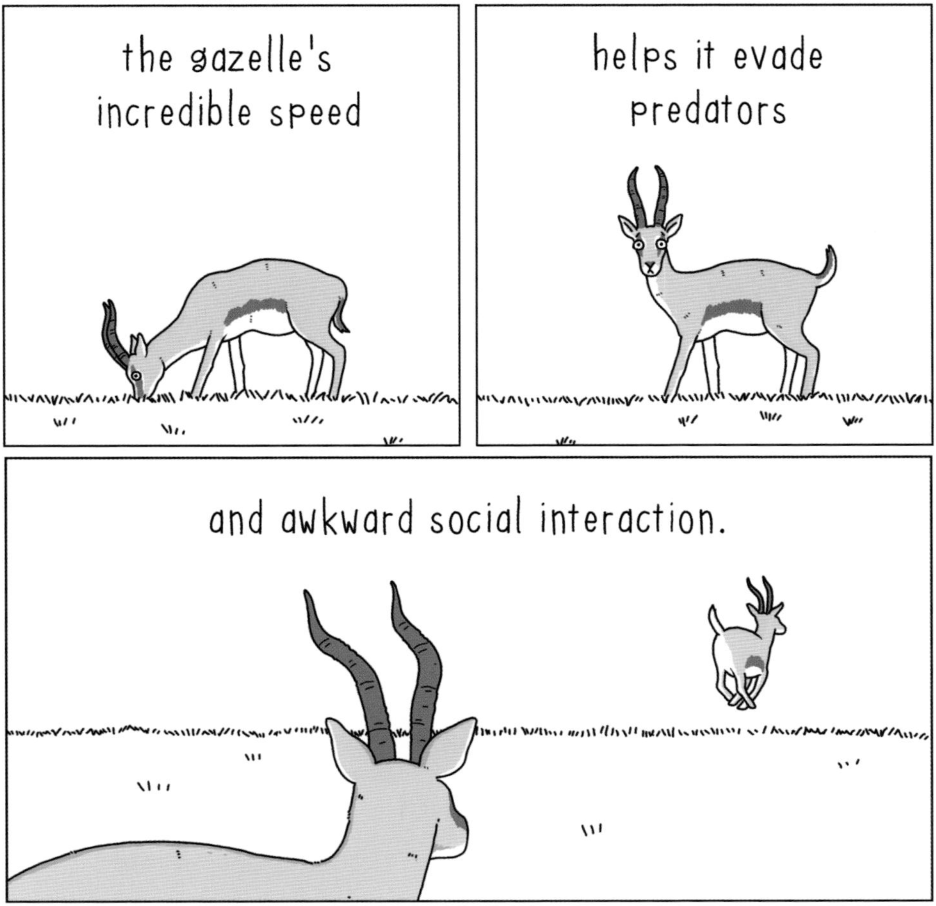
the gazelle's incredible speed
helps it evade predators
and awkward social interaction.

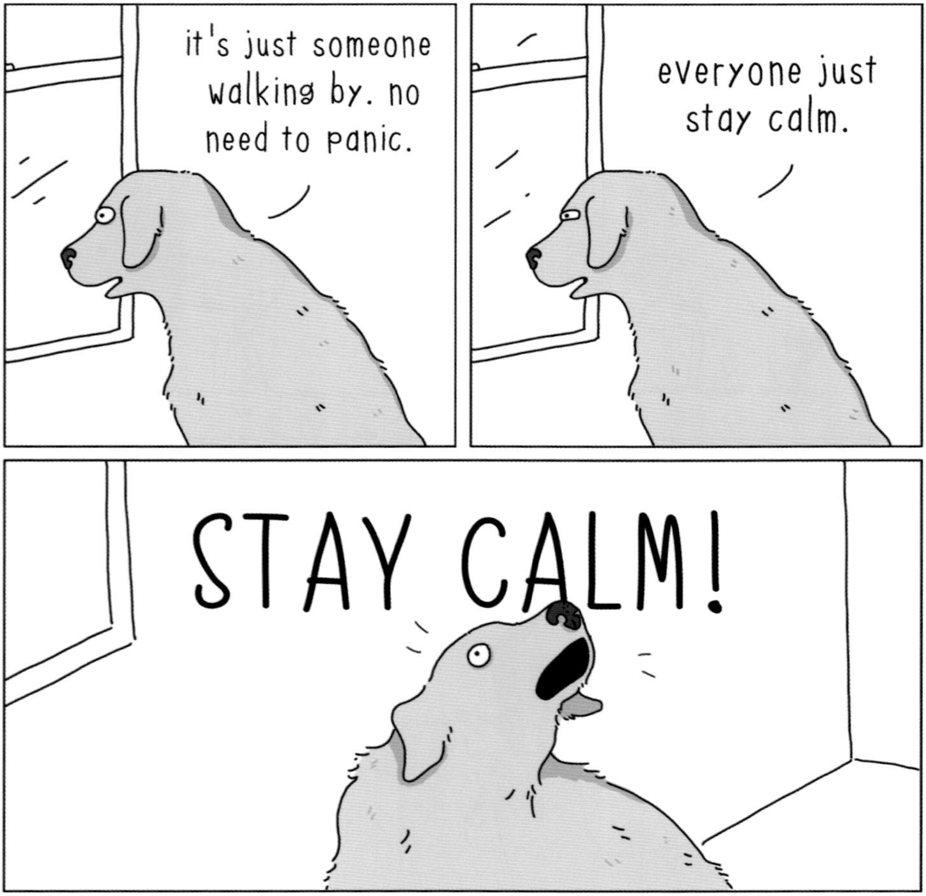
it's just someone walking by. no need to panic.
everyone just stay calm.
STAY CALM!

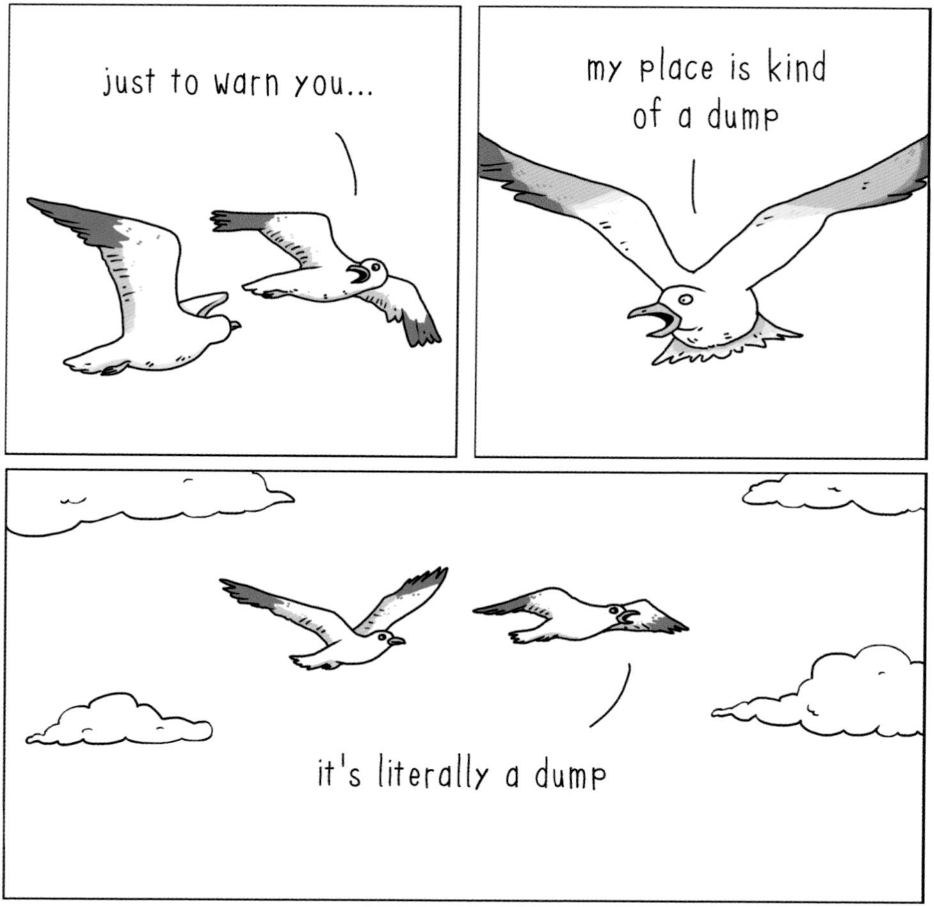
just to warn you...
my place is kind of a dump
it's literally a dump

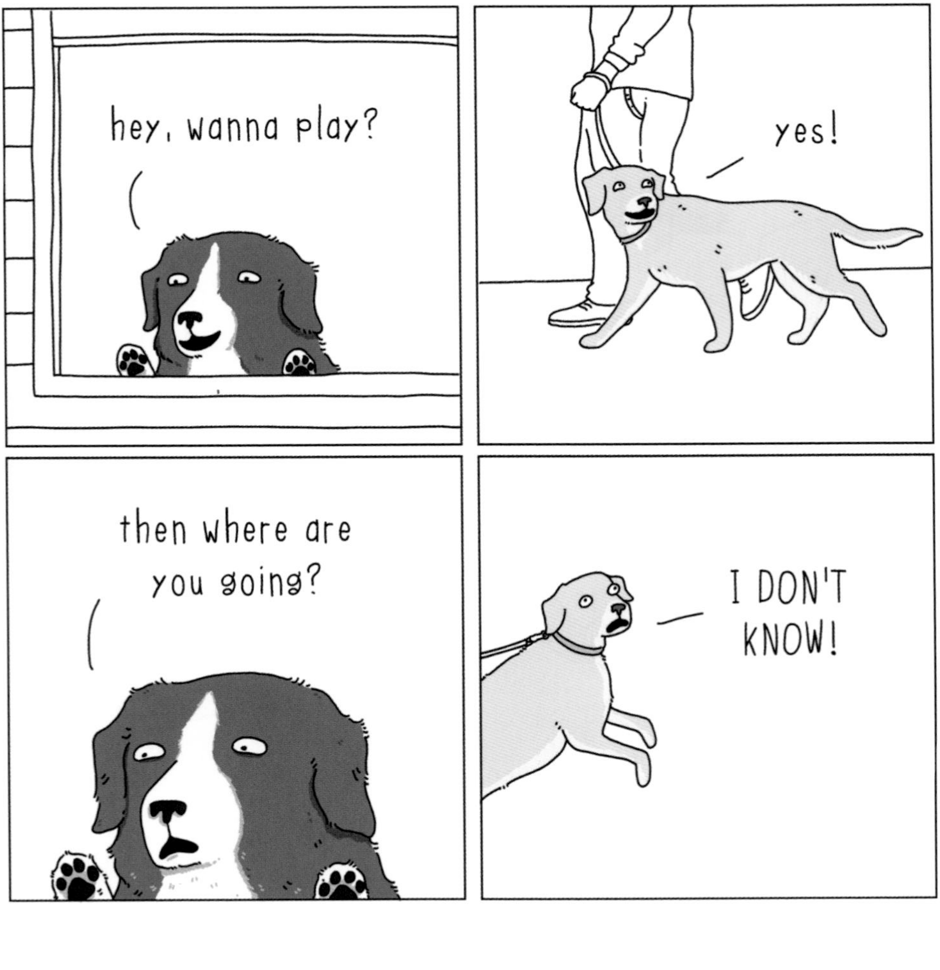
hey, wanna play?
yes!
then where are you going?
I DON'T KNOW!

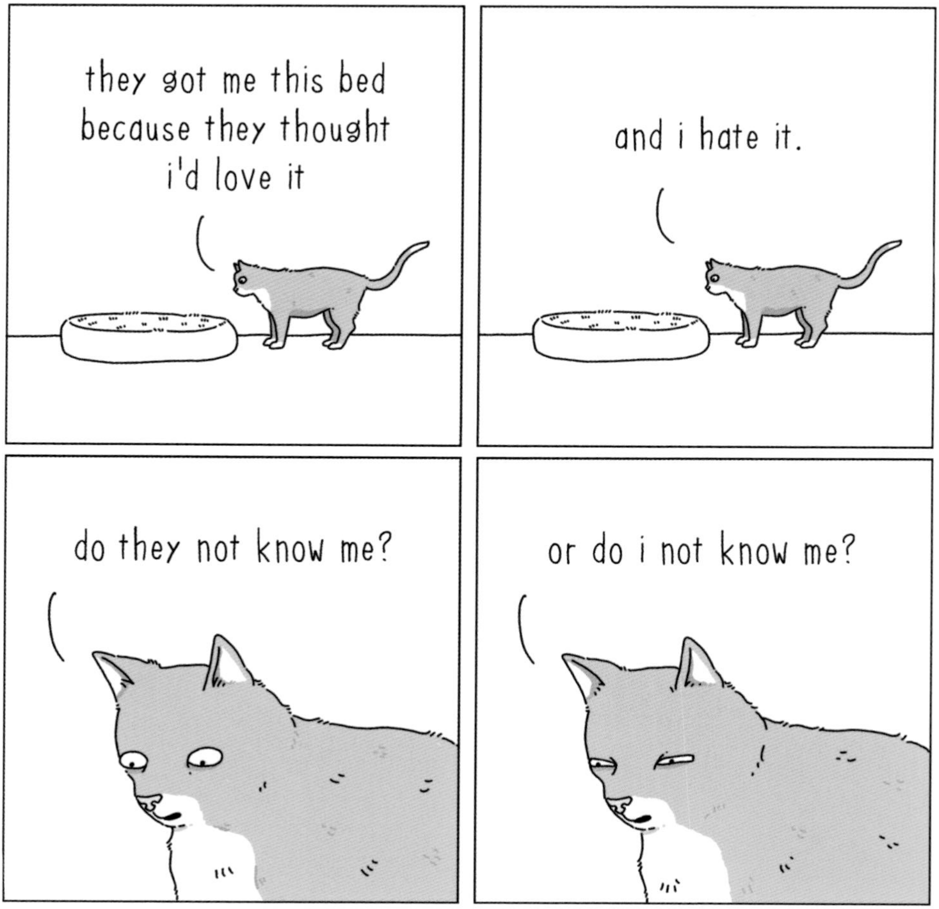
they got me this bed because they thought i'd love it
and i hate it.
do they not know me?
or do i not know me?

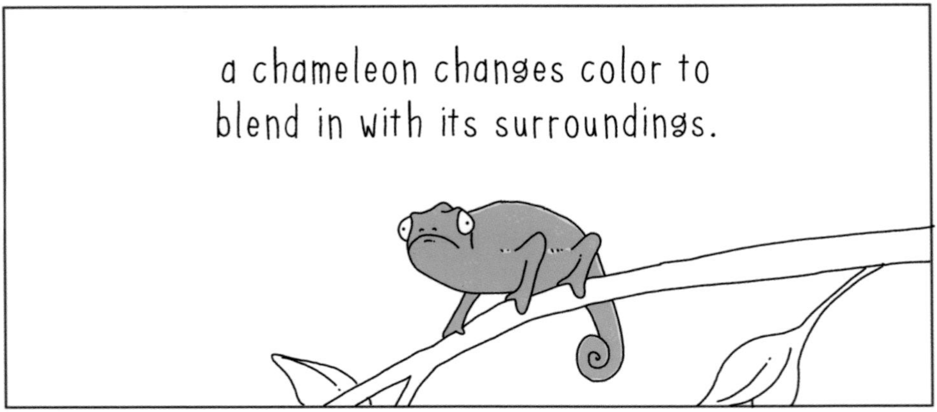
a chameleon changes color to
blend in with its surroundings.

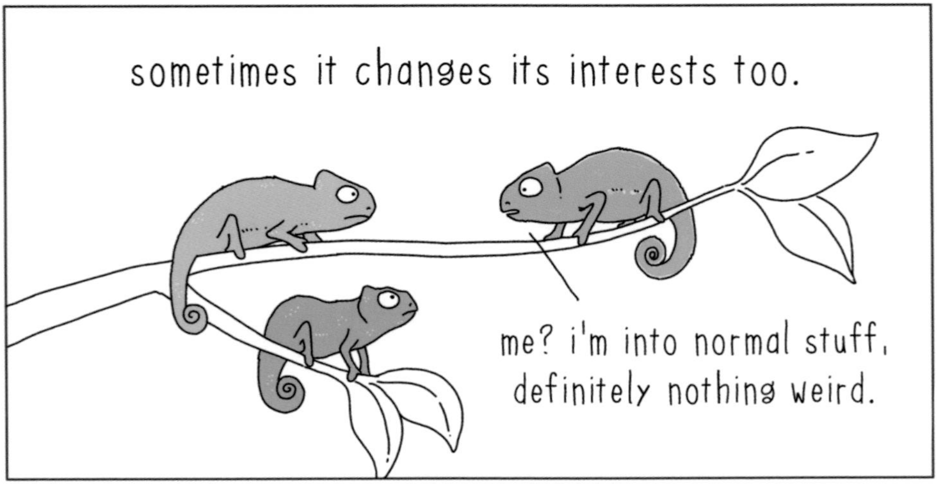
sometimes it changes its interests too.
me? i'm into normal stuff,
definitely nothing weird.

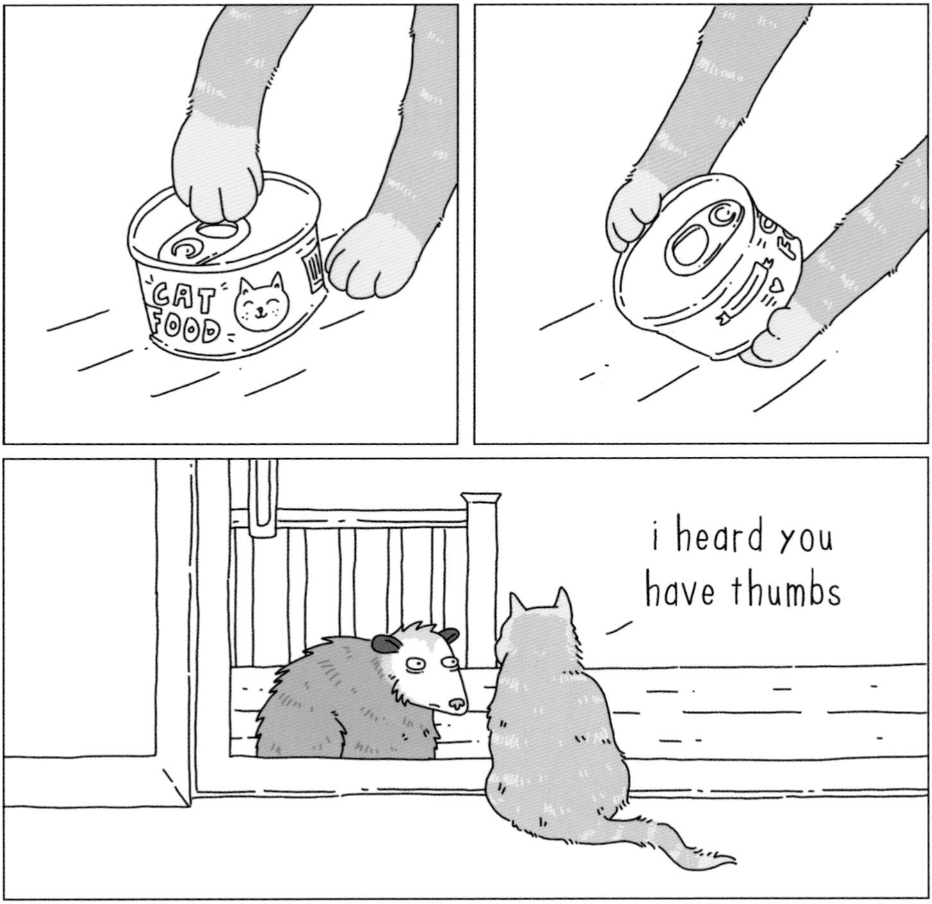
CAT FOOD
i heard you have thumbs

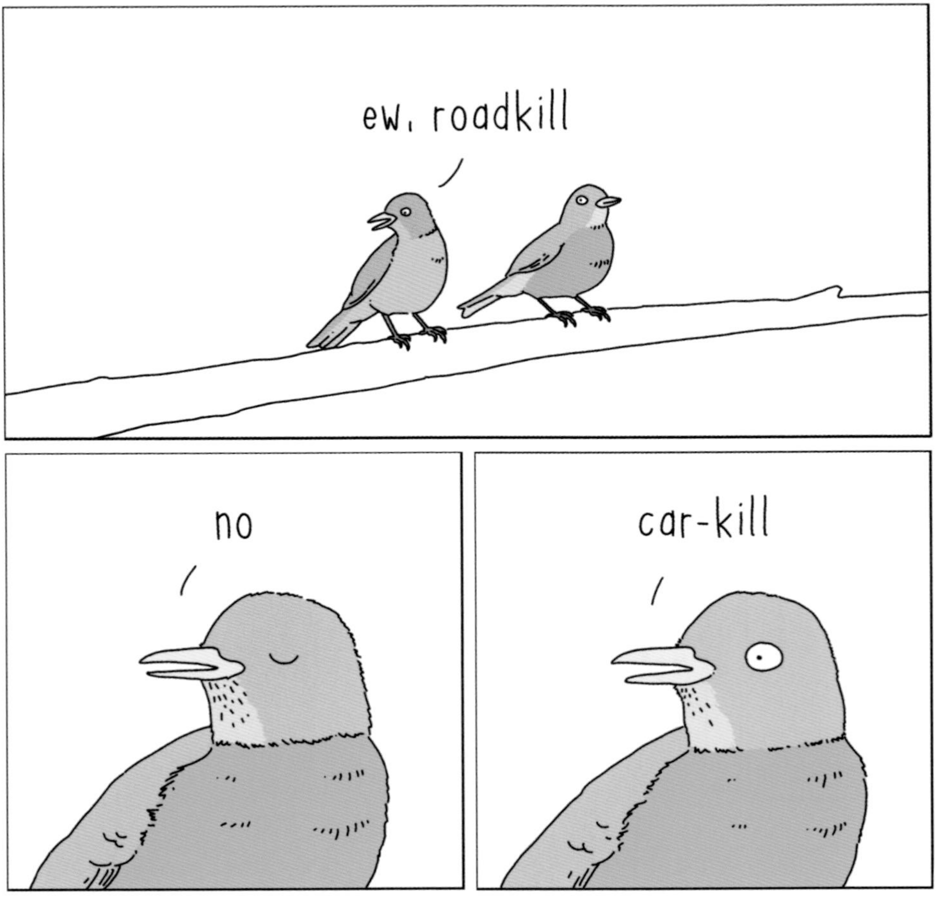
ew, roadkill
no
car-kill

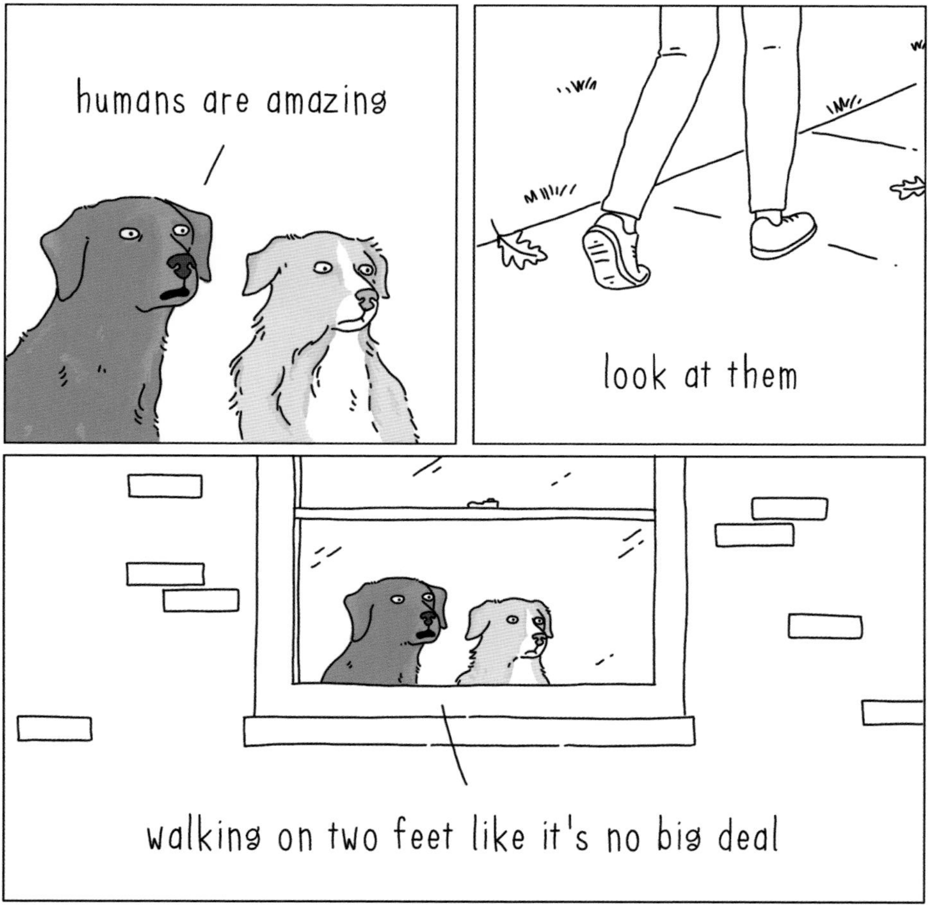
humans are amazing
look at them
walking on two feet like it's no big deal

"anteater" is like an ironic nickname, right?

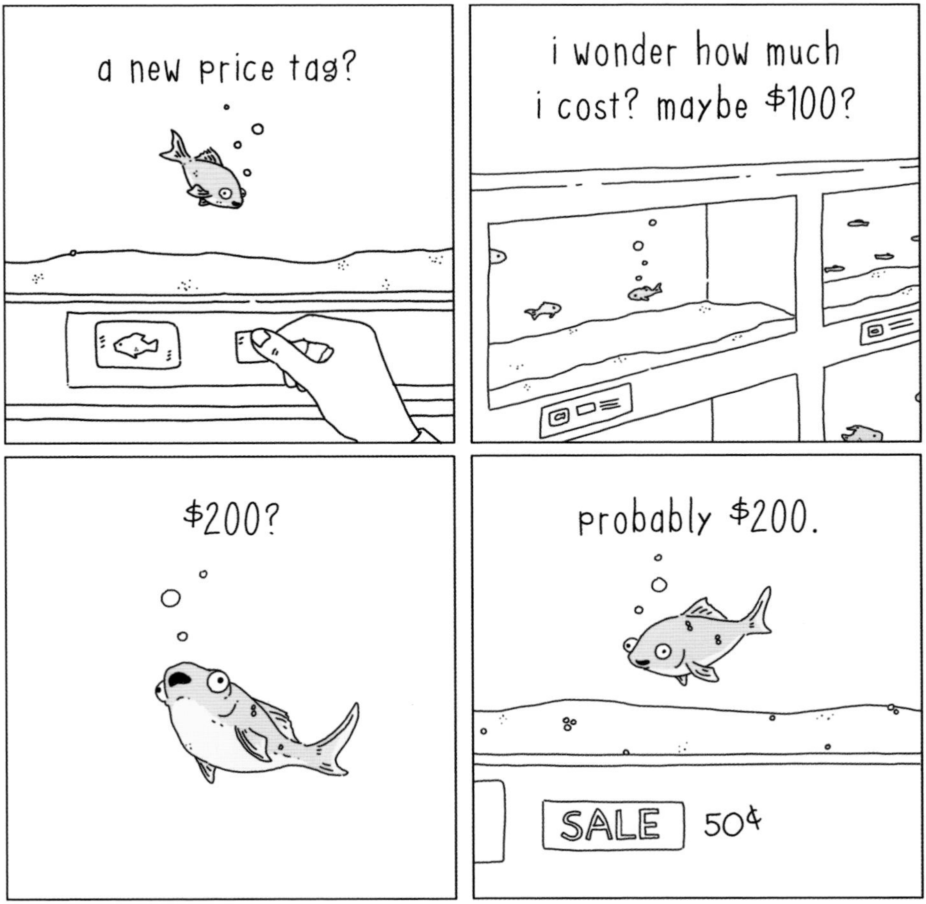
a new price tag?
i wonder how much i cost? maybe $100?
$200?
probably $200.
SALE 50¢

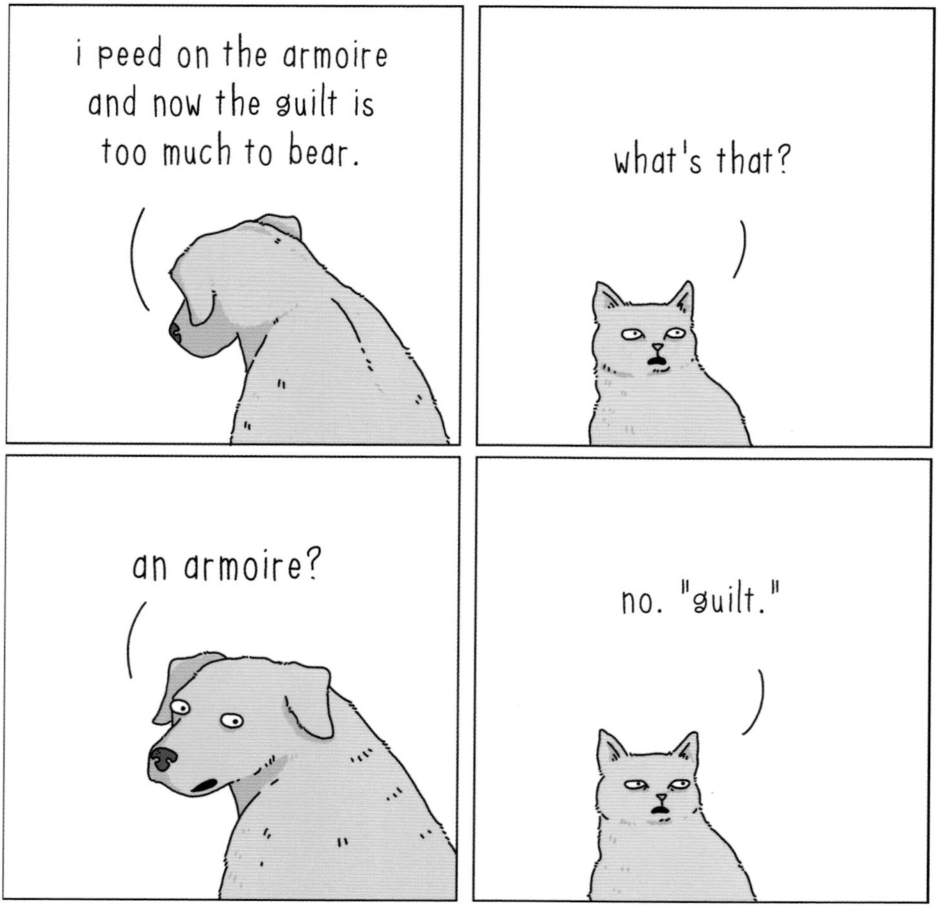
i peed on the armoire and now the guilt is too much to bear.
what's that?
an armoire?
no. "guilt."

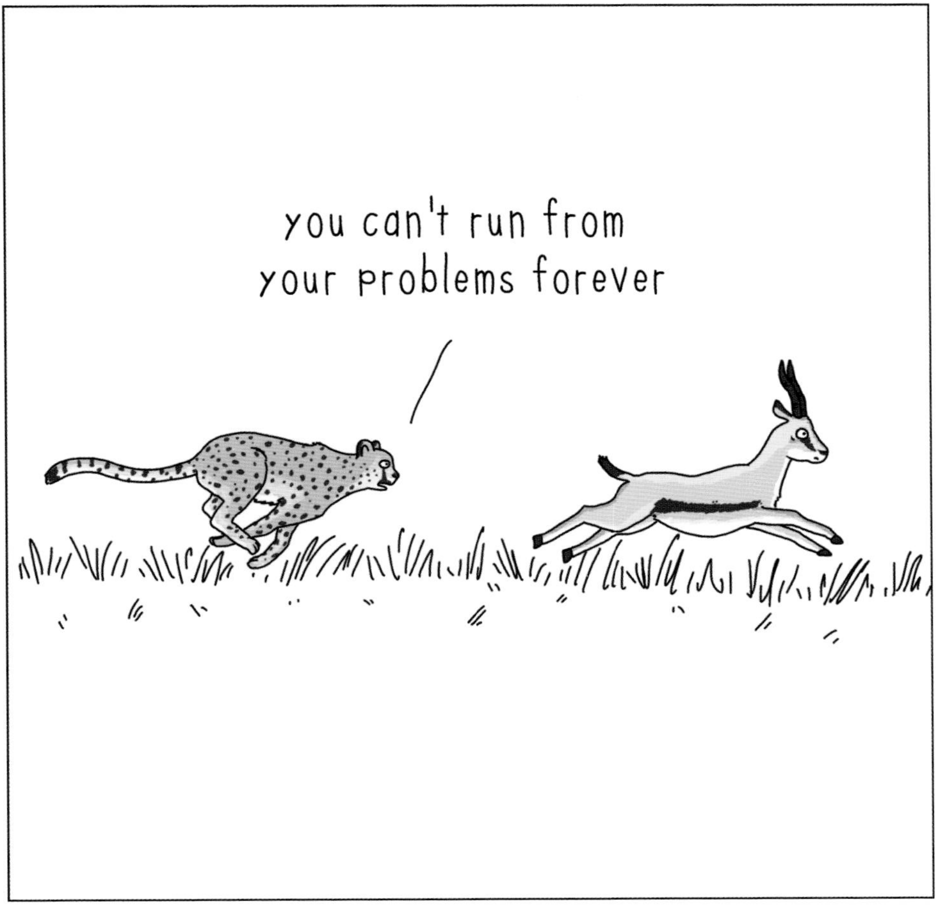
you can't run from
your problems forever

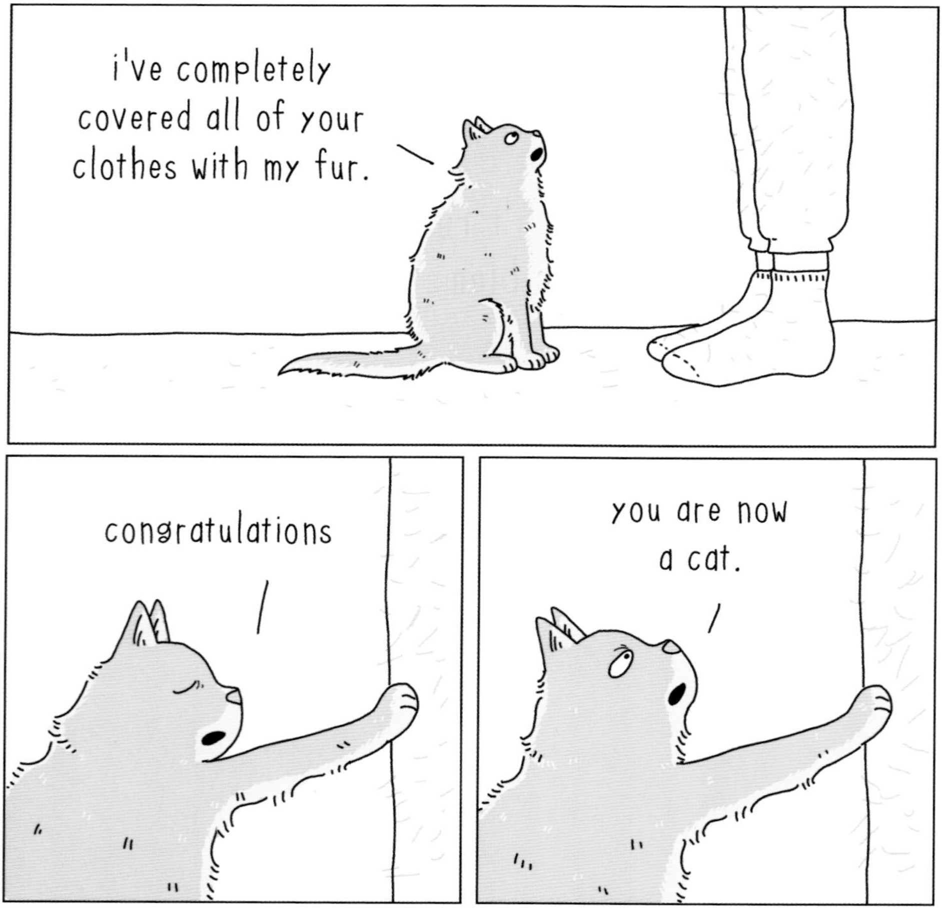
i've completely covered all of your clothes with my fur.
congratulations
you are now a cat.

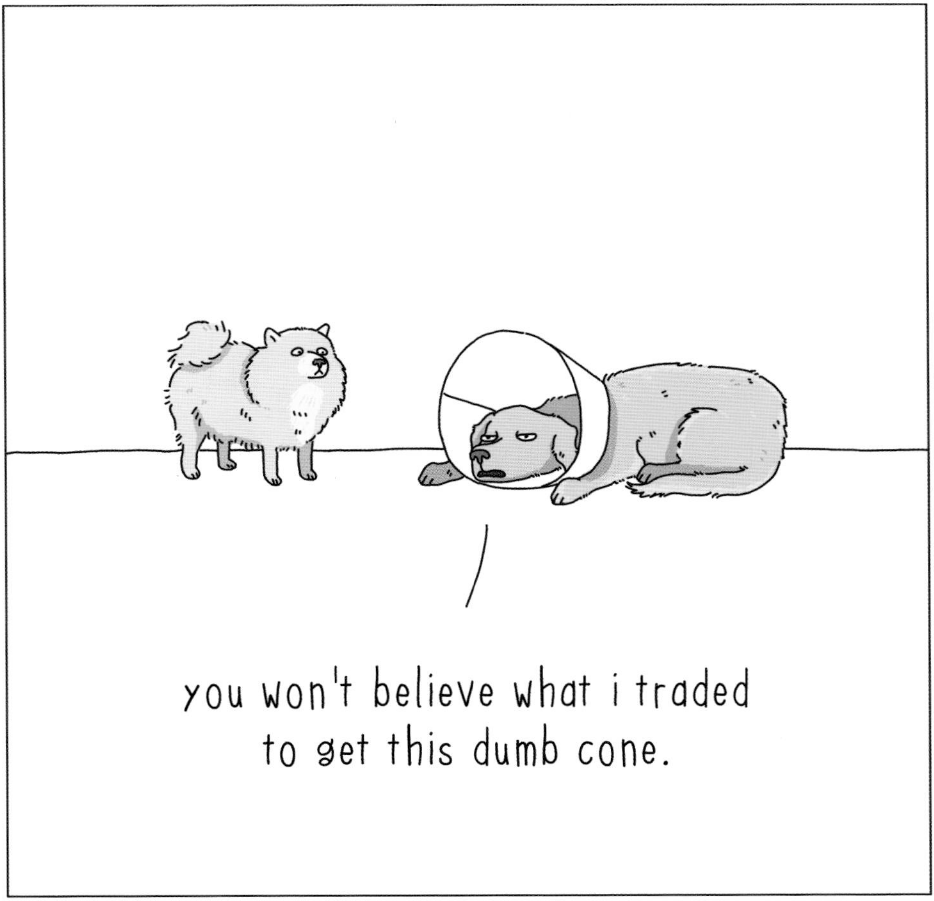
you won't believe what i traded
to get this dumb cone.

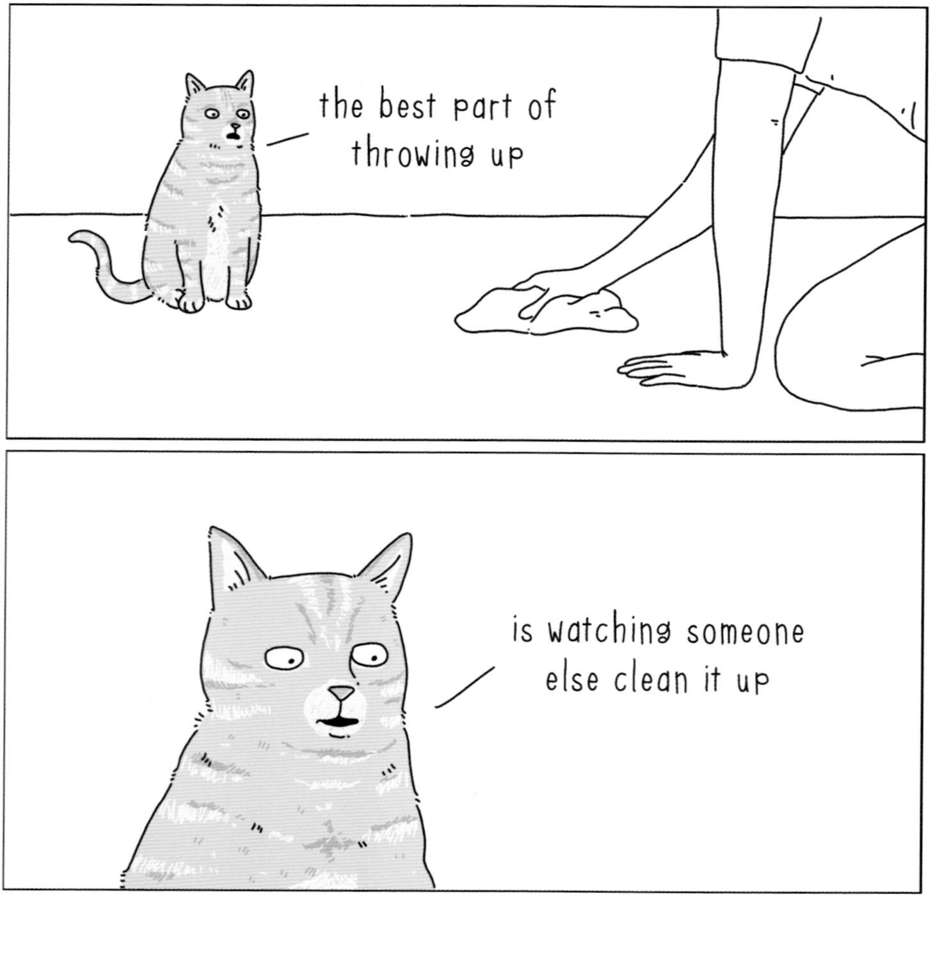
the best part of
throwing up
is watching someone
else clean it up

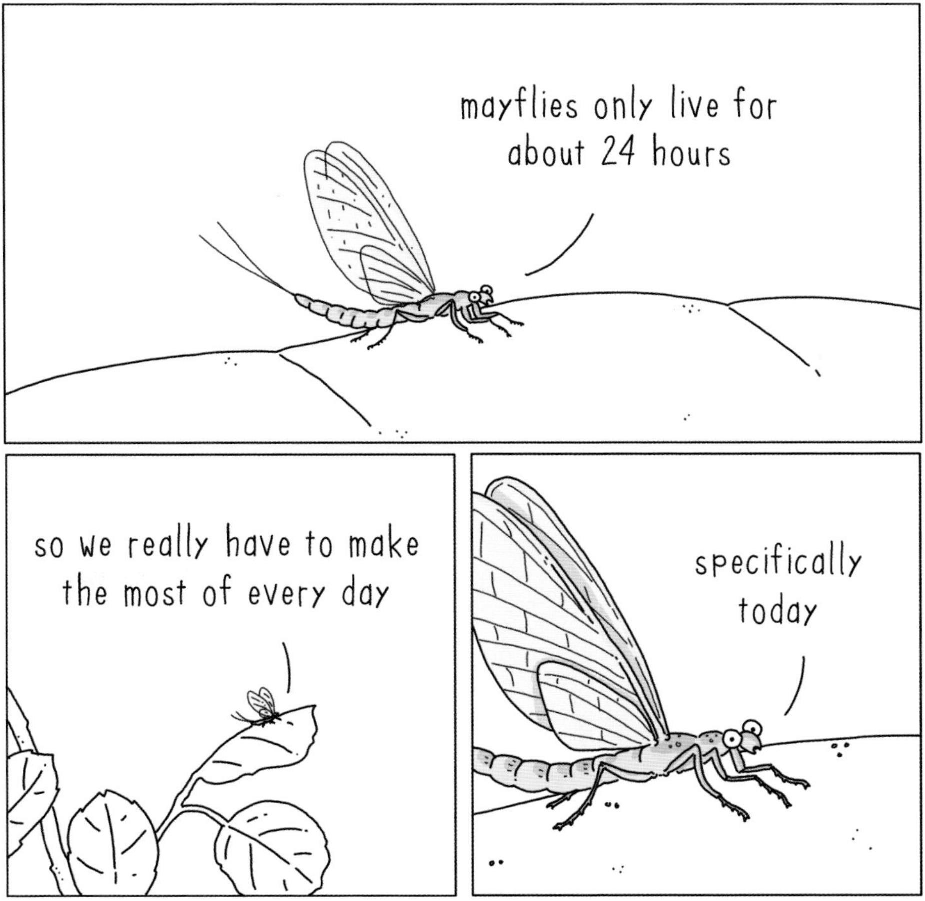
mayflies only live for about 24 hours
so we really have to make the most of every day
specifically today

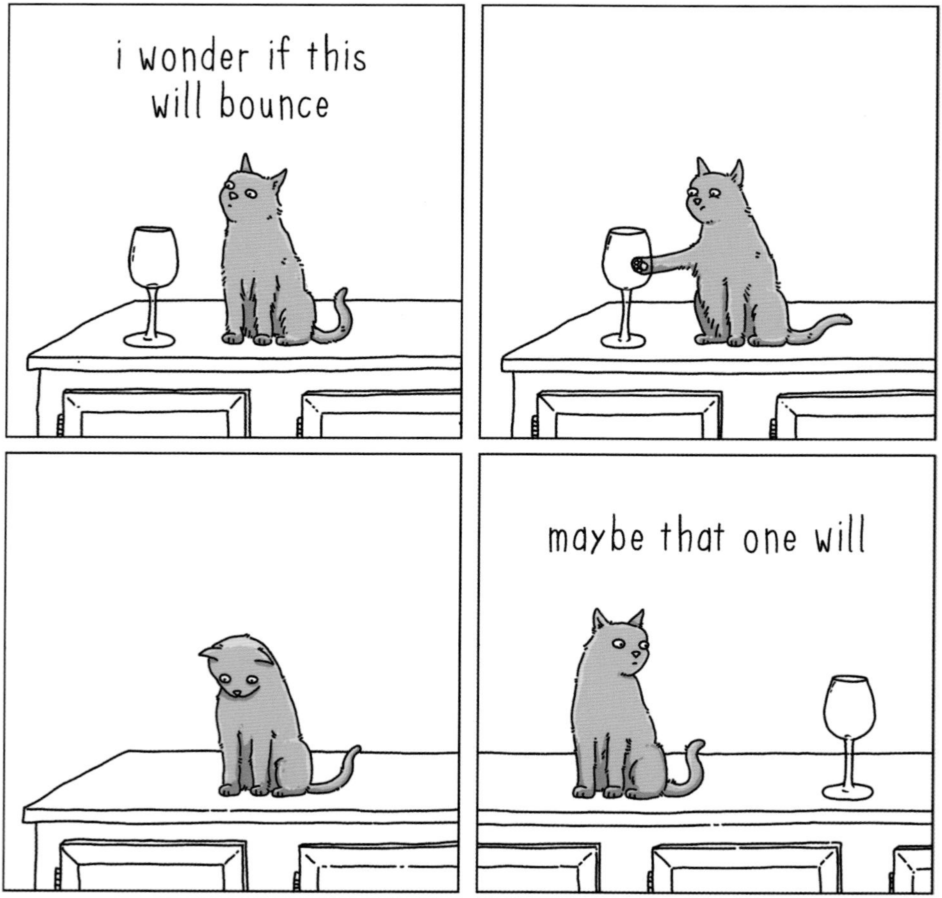
i wonder if this will bounce
maybe that one will

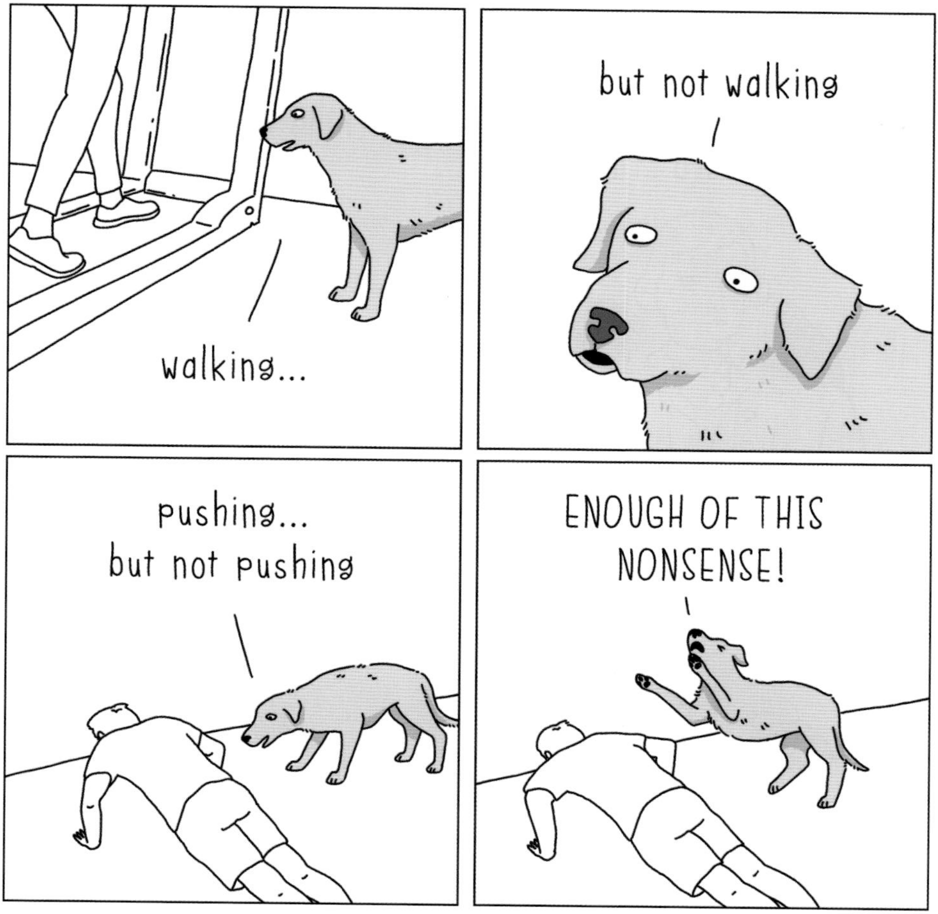
walking...
but not walking
pushing...
but not pushing
ENOUGH OF THIS NONSENSE!

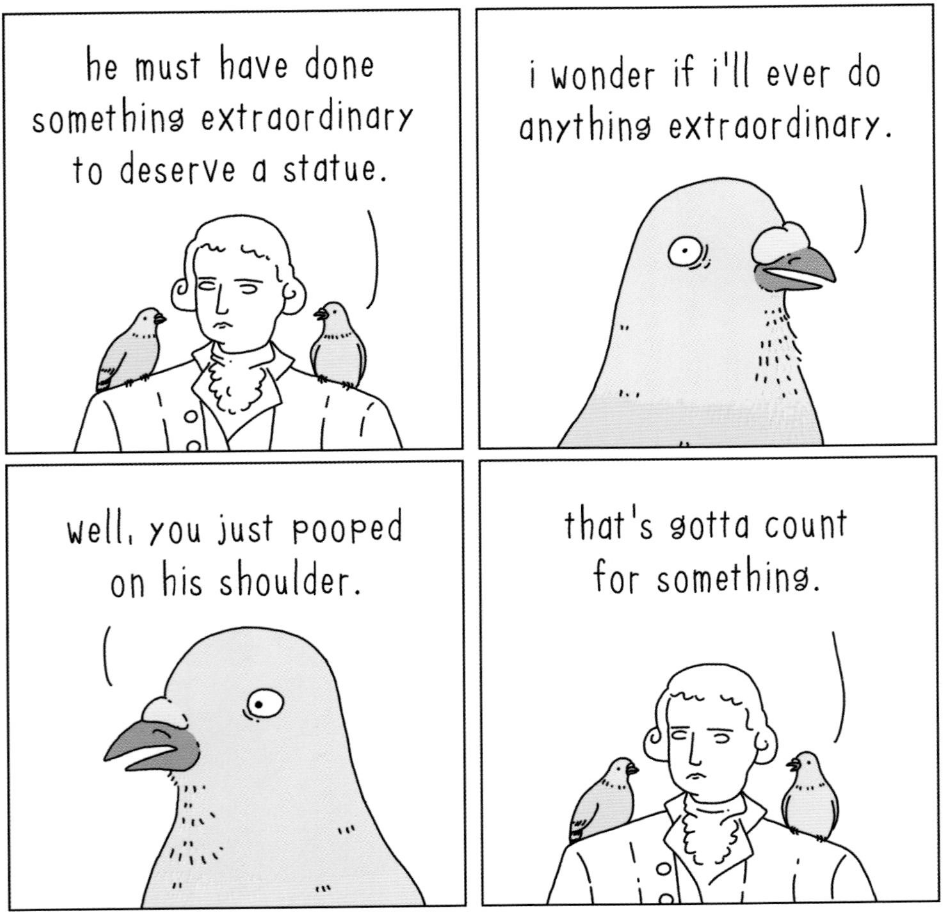
he must have done something extraordinary to deserve a statue.
i wonder if i'll ever do anything extraordinary.
well, you just pooped on his shoulder.
that's gotta count for something.

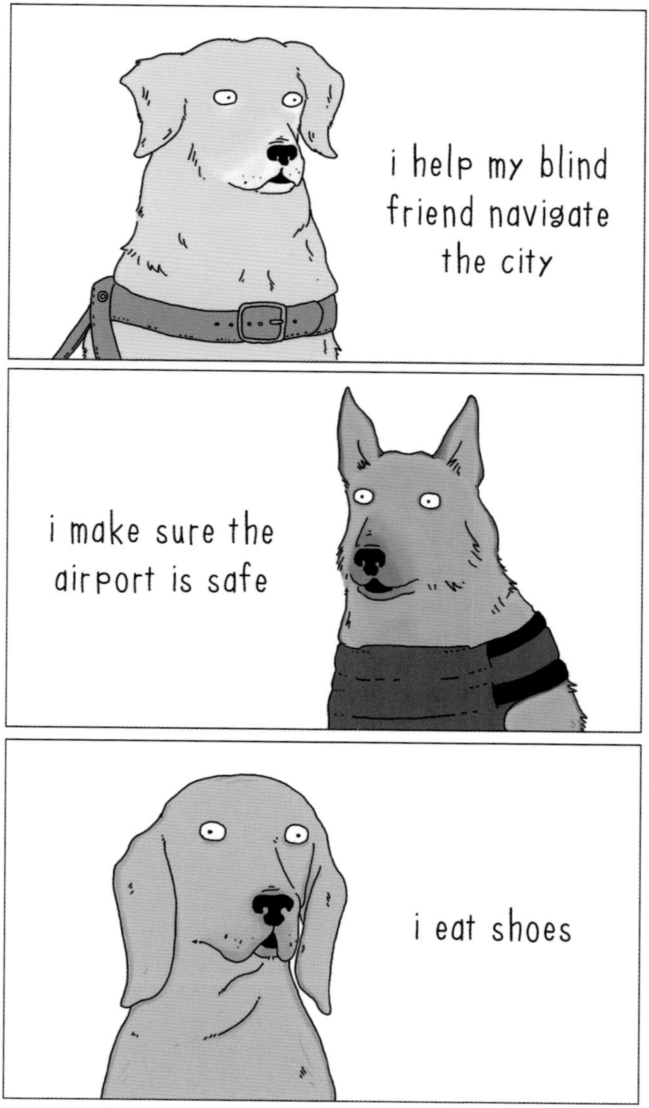
i help my blind friend navigate the city
i make sure the airport is safe
i eat shoes

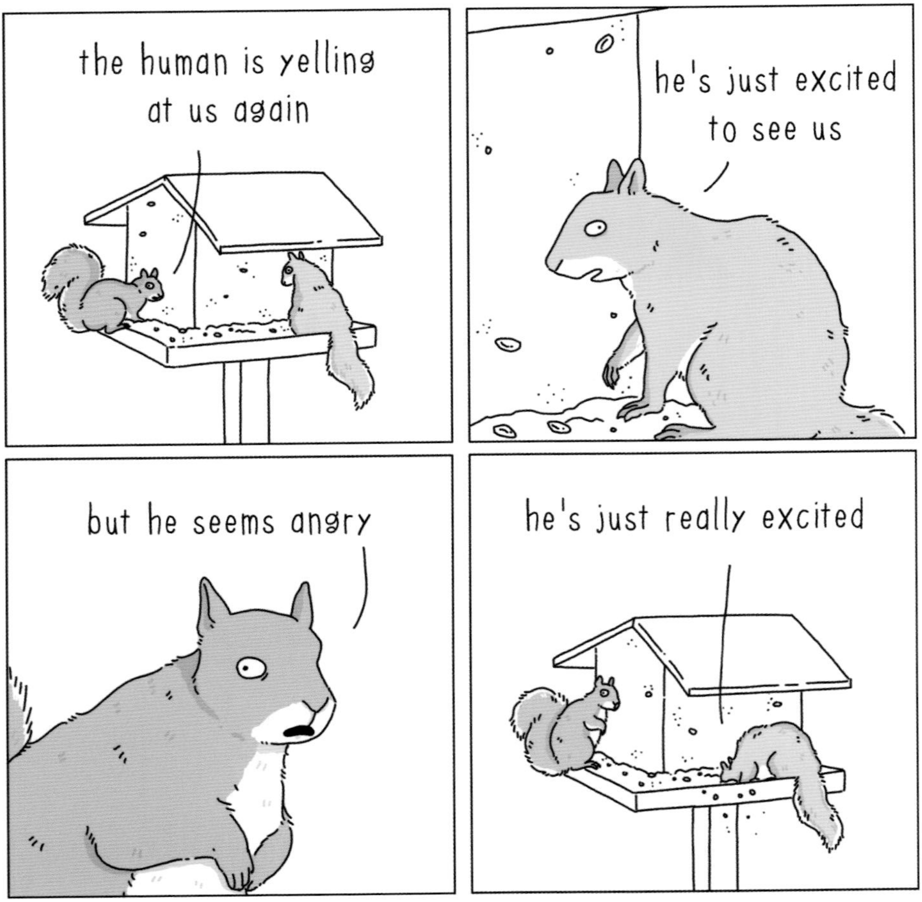
the human is yelling at us again
he's just excited to see us
but he seems angry
he's just really excited

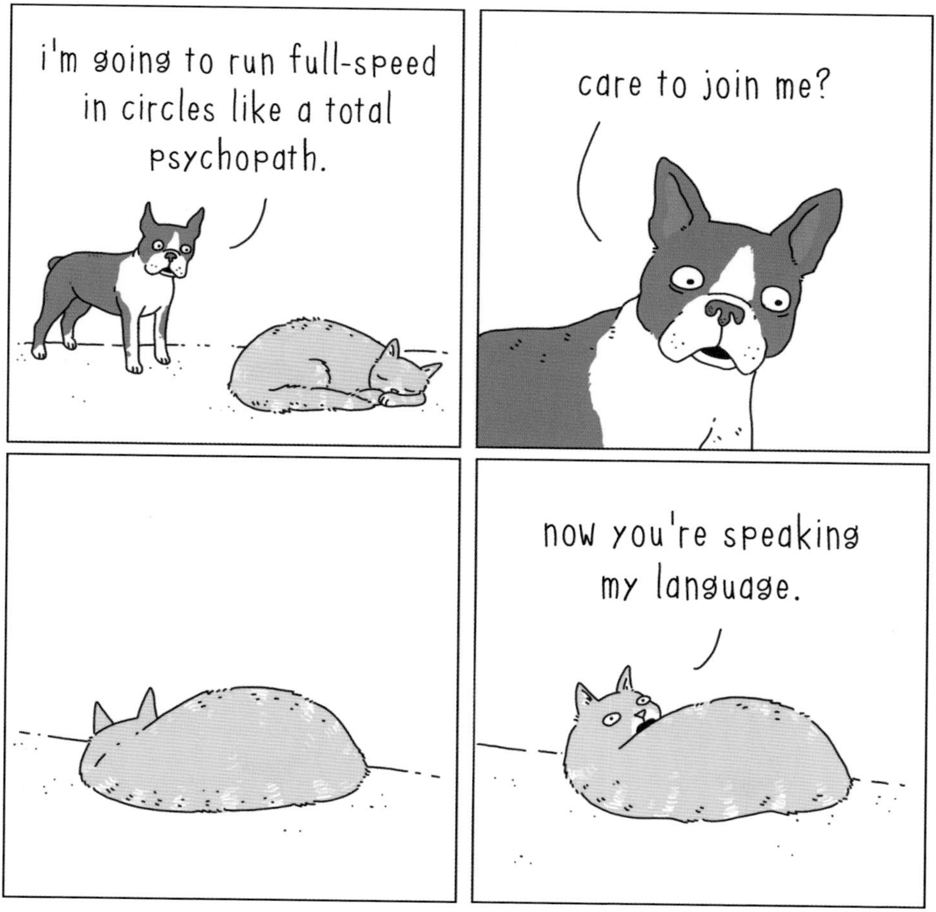

i'm going to run full-speed in circles like a total psychopath.
care to join me?
now you're speaking my language.

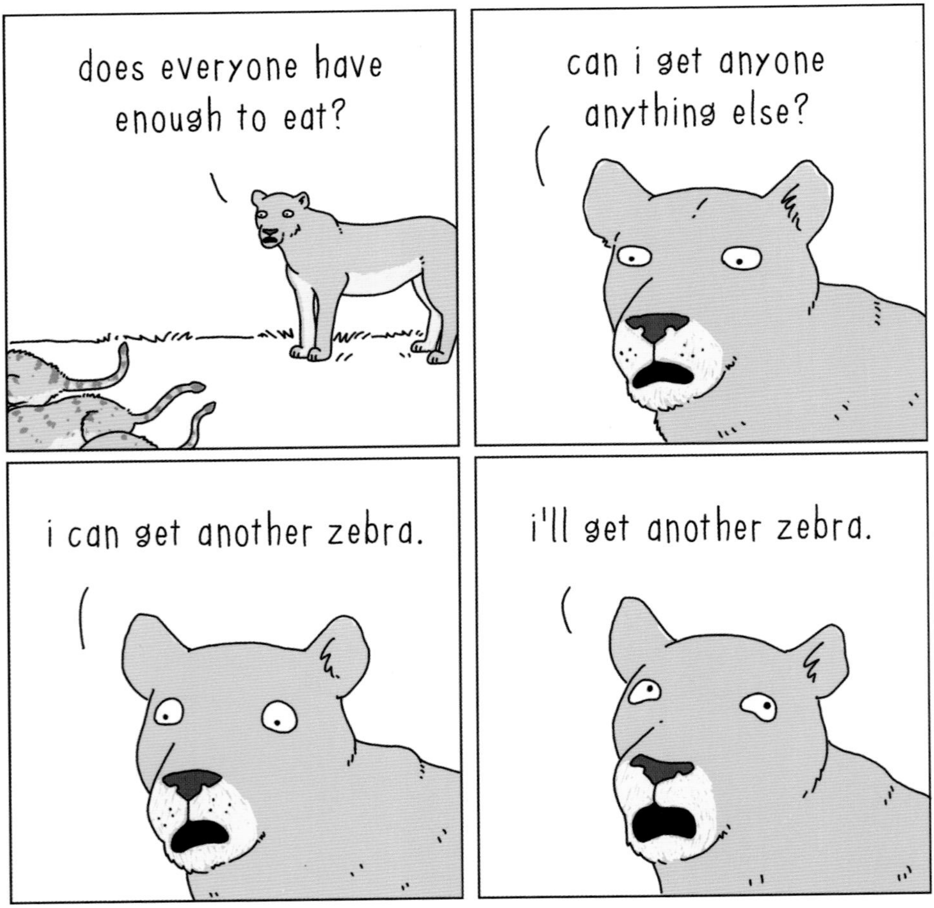
does everyone have enough to eat?
can i get anyone anything else?
i can get another zebra.
i'll get another zebra.

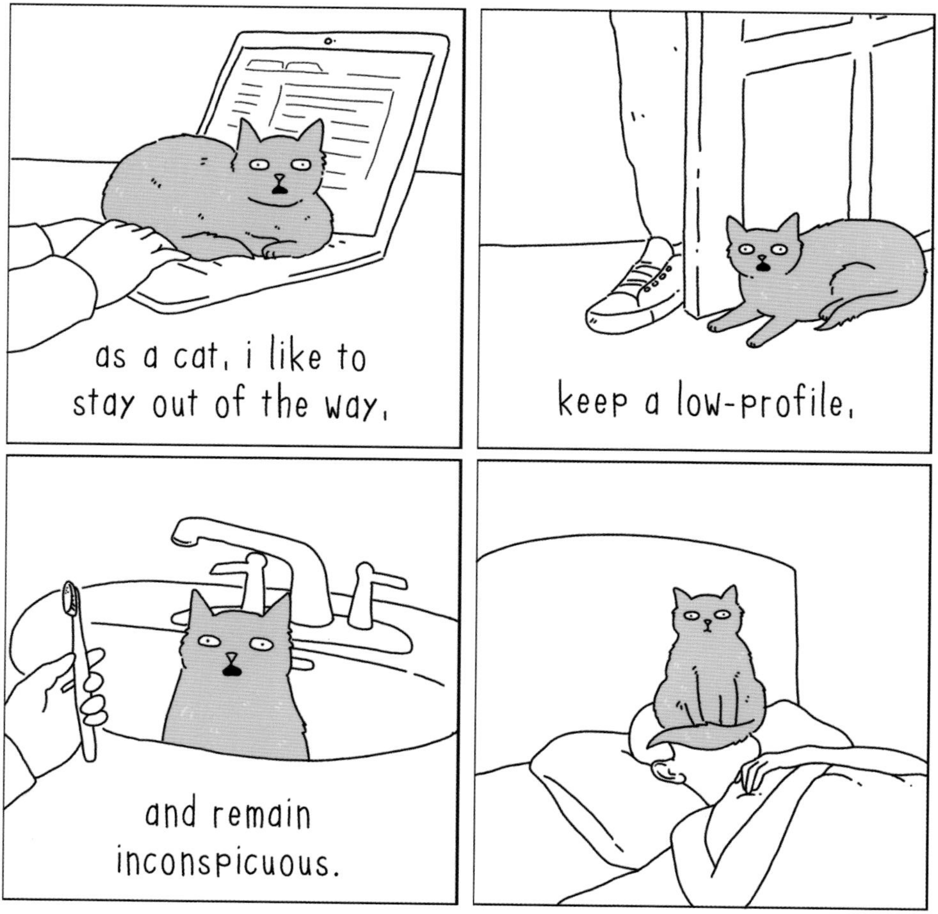
as a cat, i like to stay out of the way,
keep a low-profile,
and remain inconspicuous.

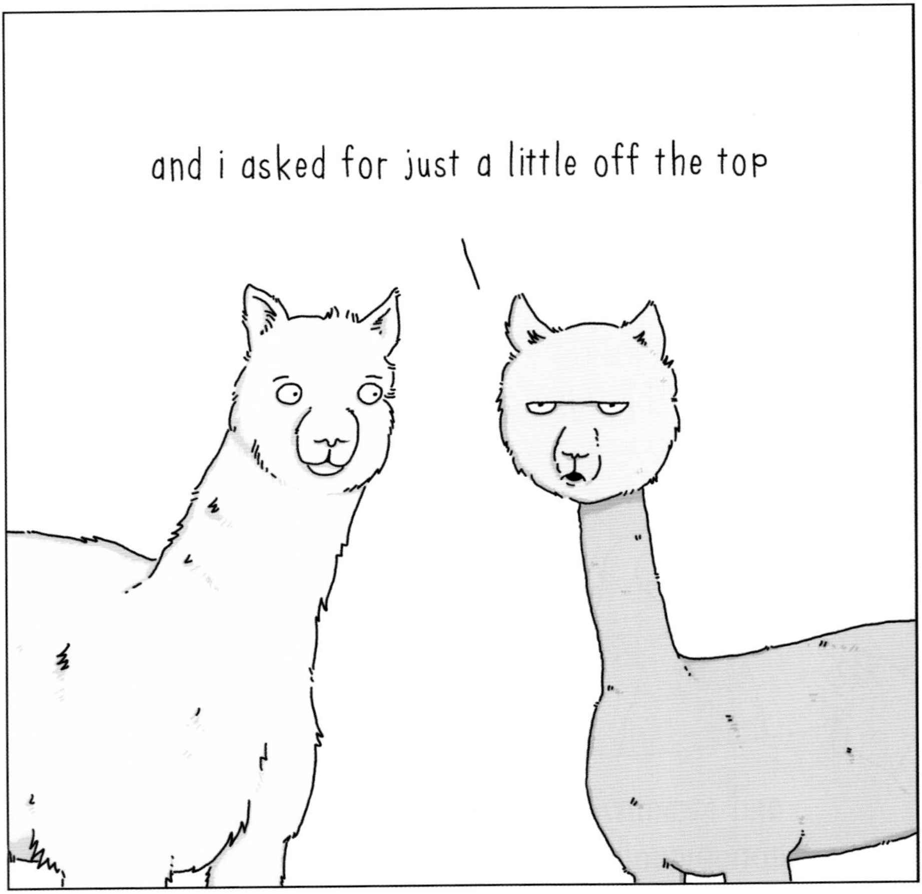
and i asked for just a little off the top

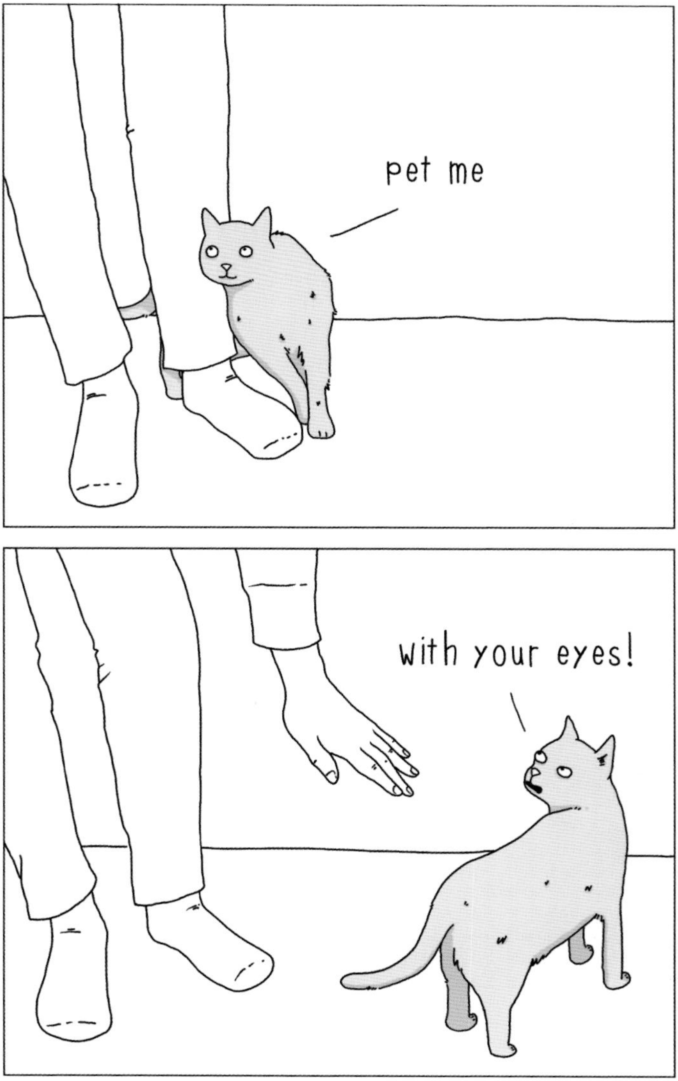
pet me
with your eyes!

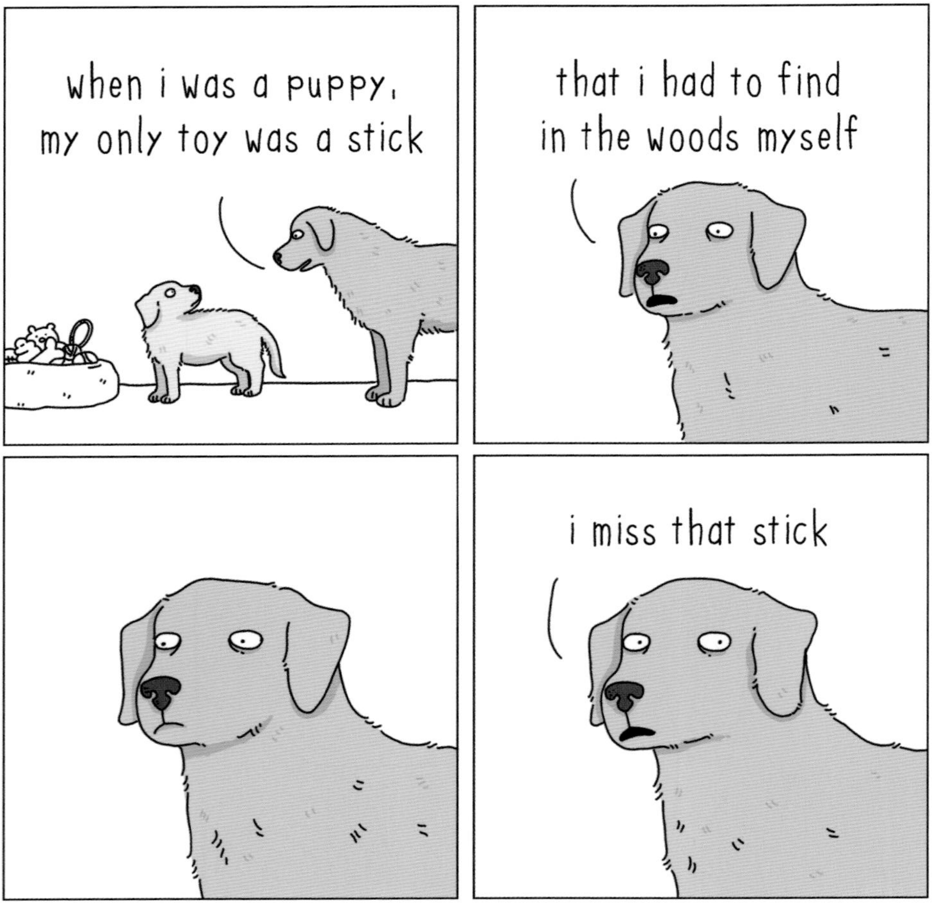
when i was a puppy,
my only toy was a stick
that i had to find
in the woods myself
i miss that stick

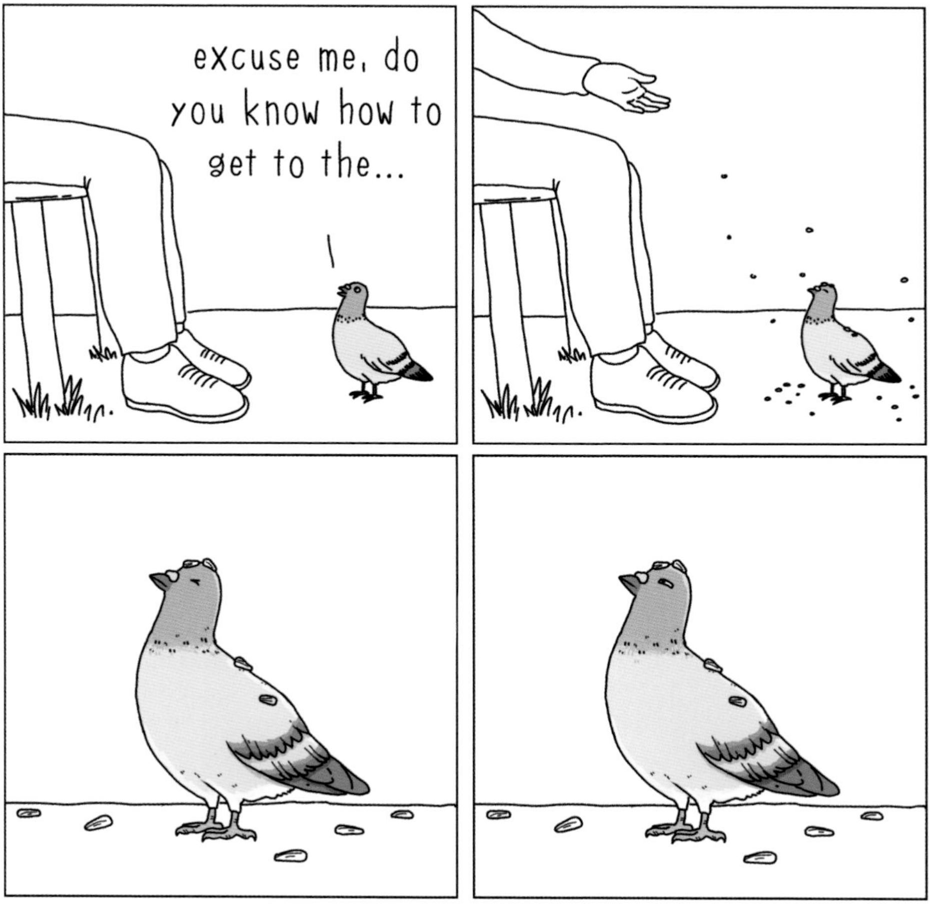
excuse me, do you know how to get to the...

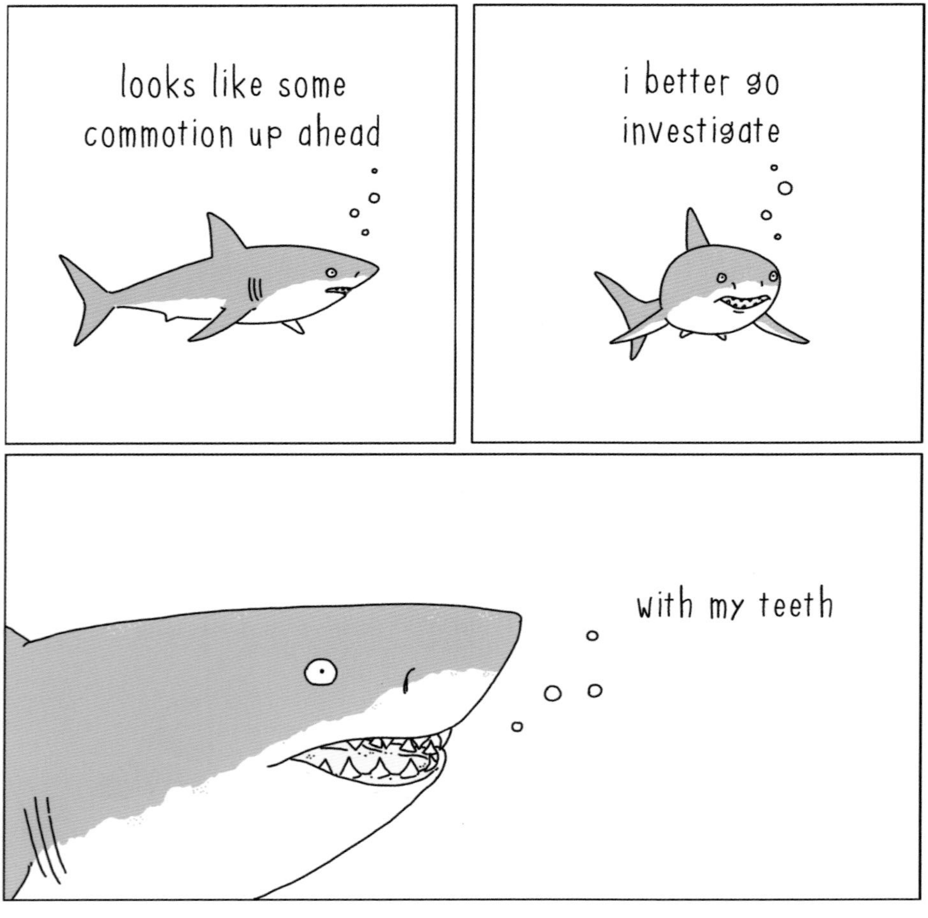
looks like some commotion up ahead
i better go investigate
with my teeth

hah, this tail has a little face.

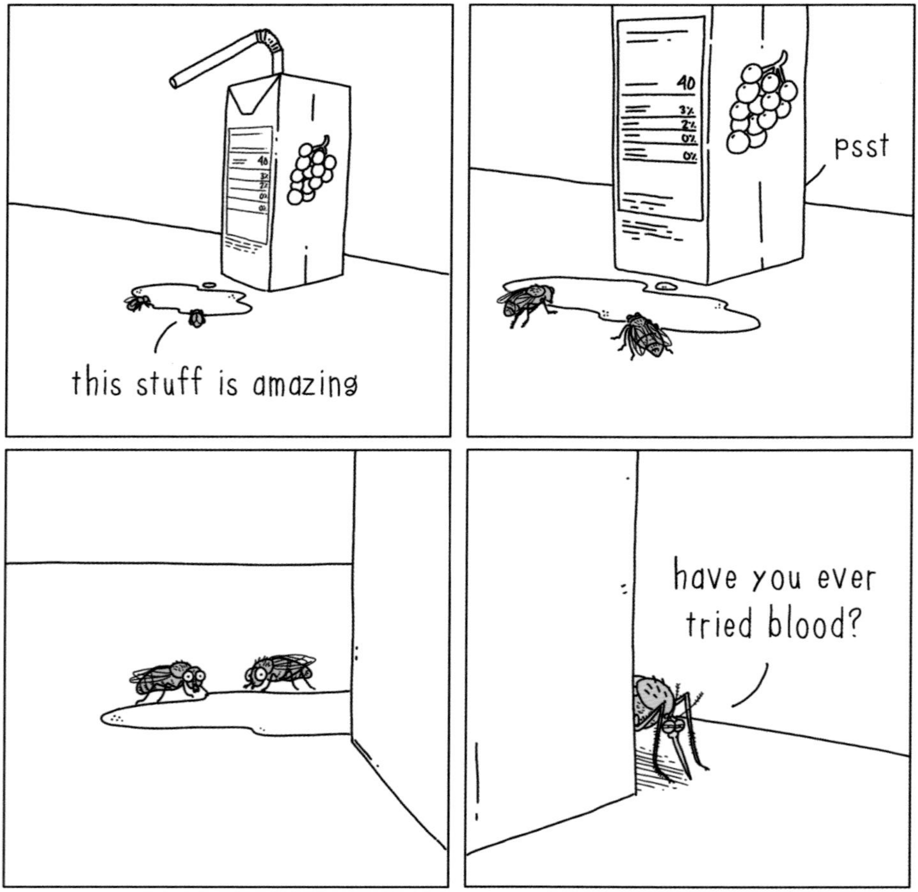
this stuff is amazing
psst
have you ever tried blood?

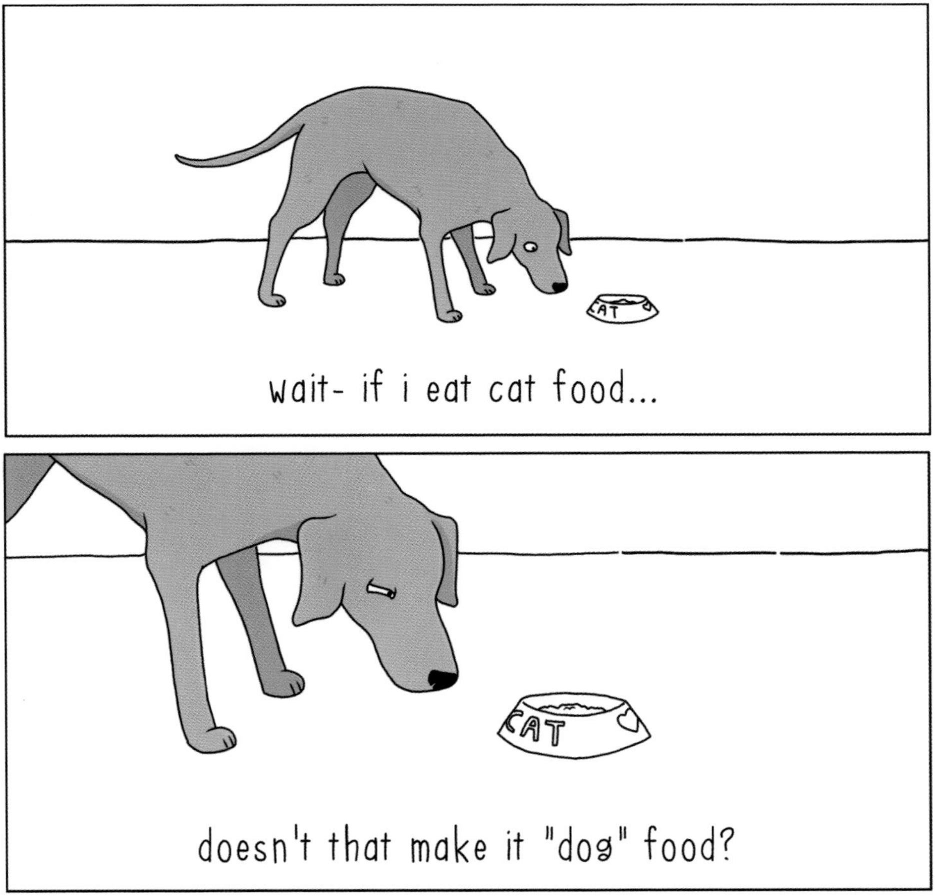
CAT
wait- if i eat cat food...
CAT
doesn't that make it "dog" food?

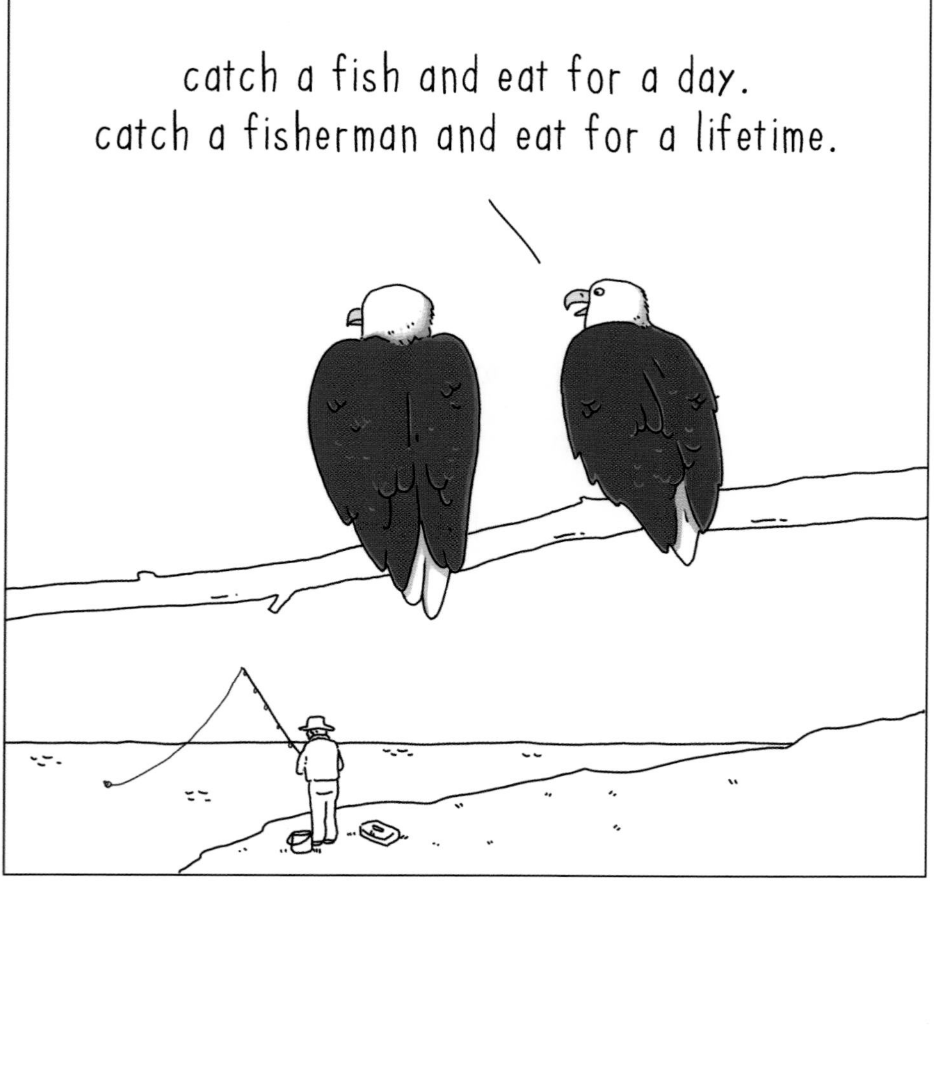
catch a fish and eat for a day.
catch a fisherman and eat for a lifetime.

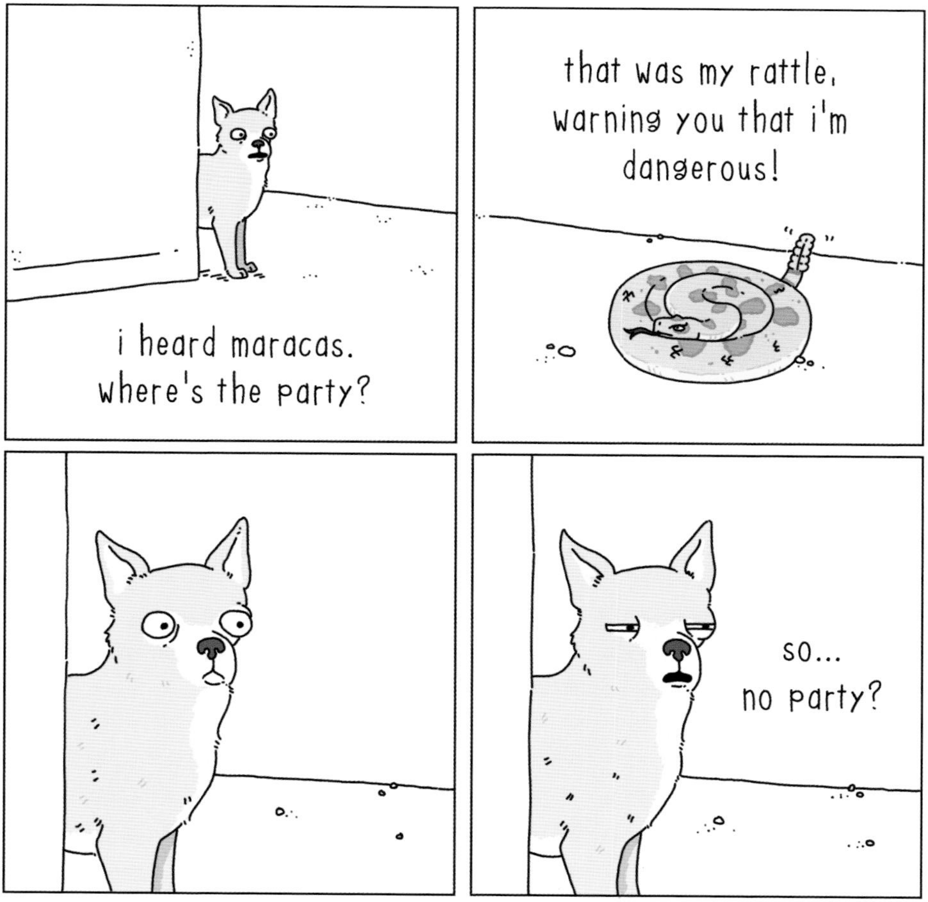
i heard maracas.
where's the party?
that was my rattle,
warning you that i'm
dangerous!
so...
no party?

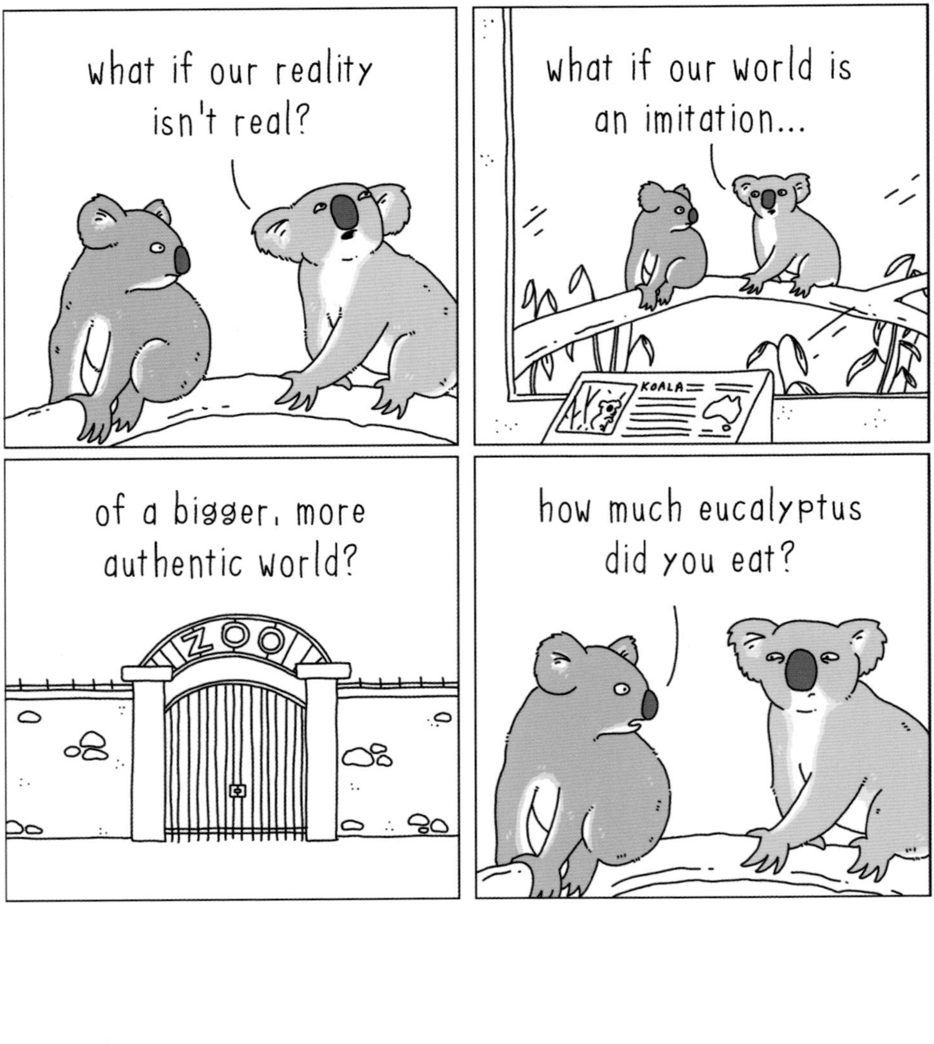
what if our reality isn't real?
what if our world is an imitation...
KOALA
of a bigger, more authentic world?
ZOO
how much eucalyptus did you eat?

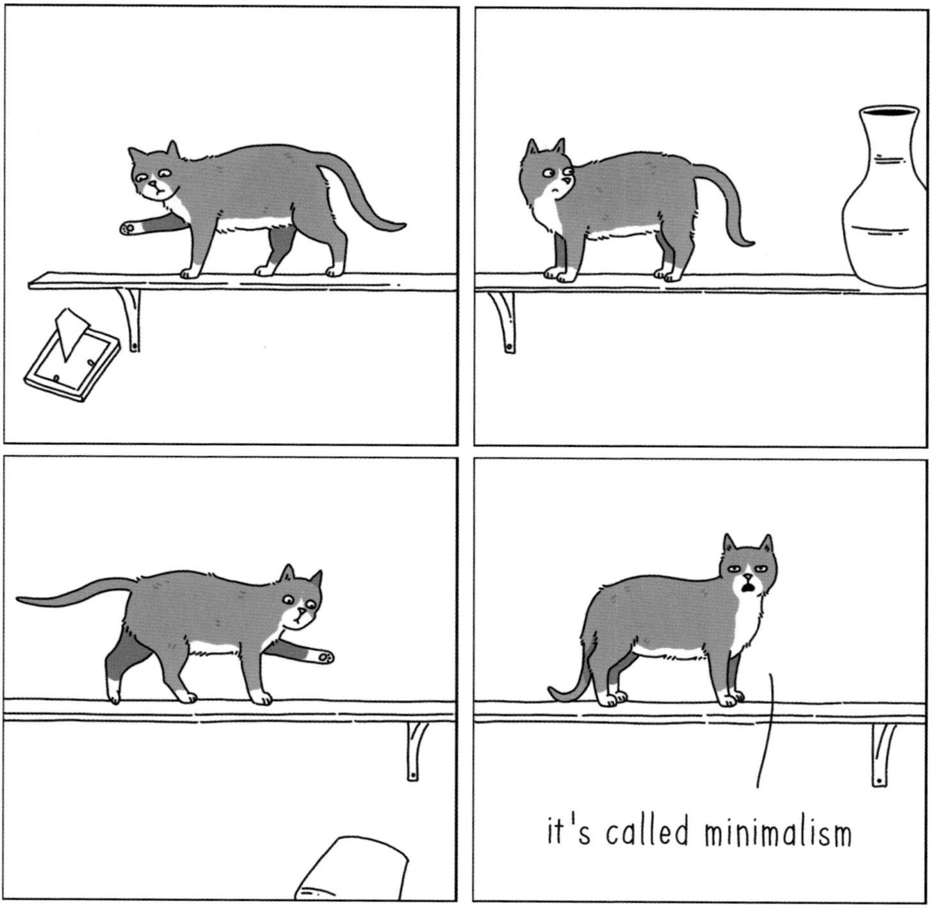
it's called minimalism

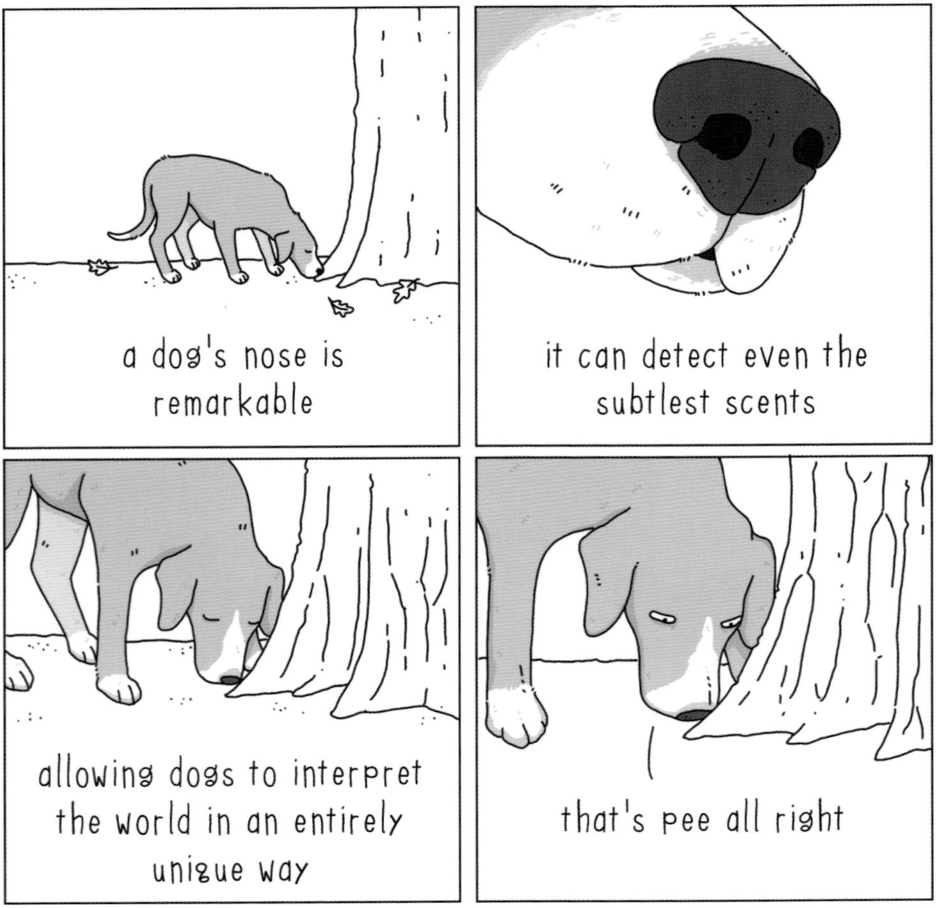
a dog's nose is remarkable
it can detect even the subtlest scents
allowing dogs to interpret the world in an entirely unique way
that's pee all right

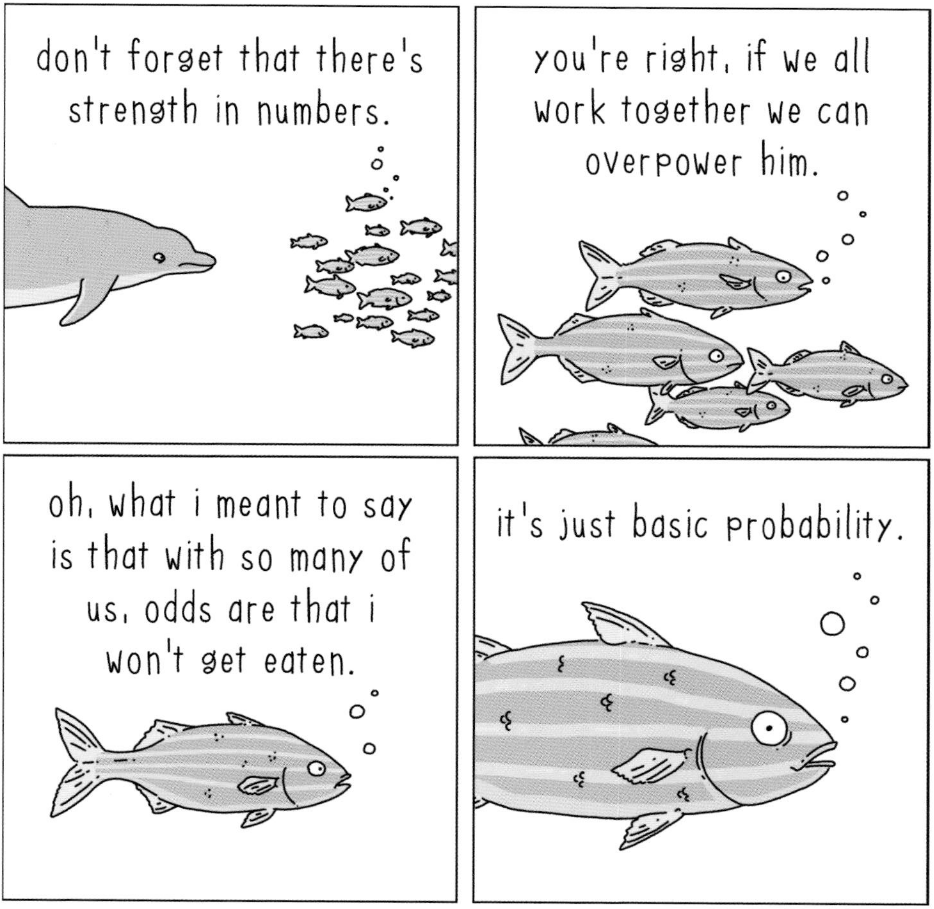
don't forget that there's strength in numbers.
you're right, if we all work together we can overpower him.
oh, what i meant to say is that with so many of us, odds are that i won't get eaten.
it's just basic probability.

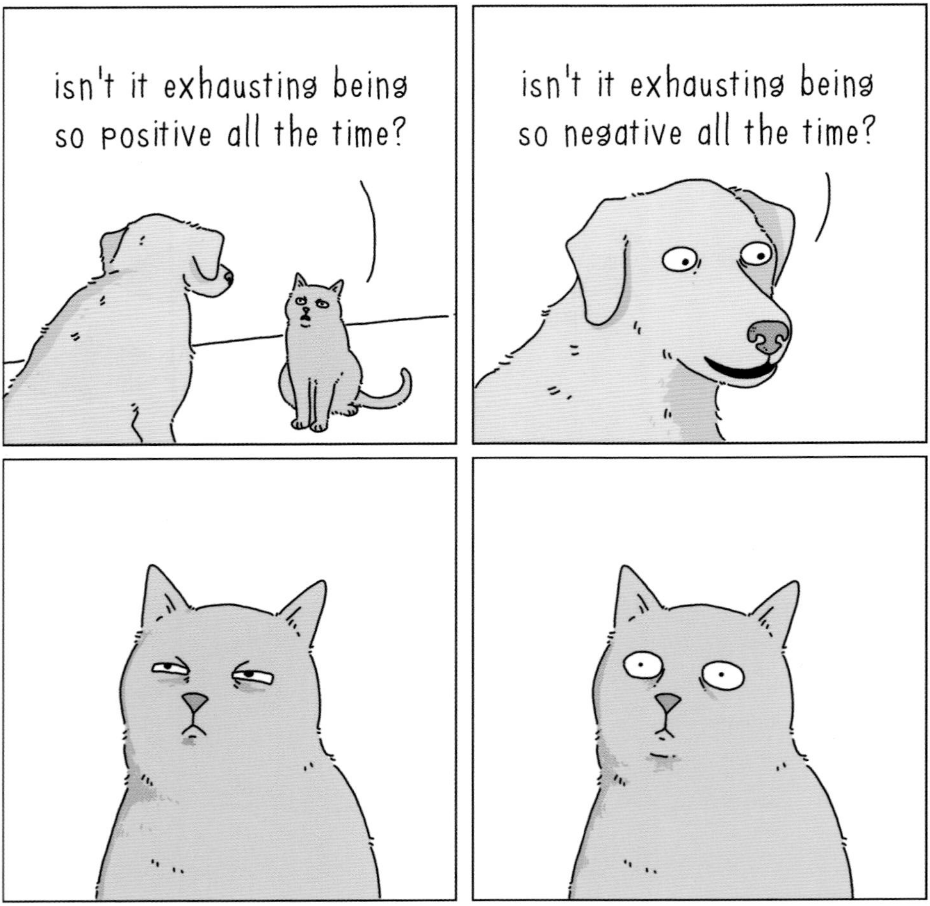
isn't it exhausting being so positive all the time?
isn't it exhausting being so negative all the time?

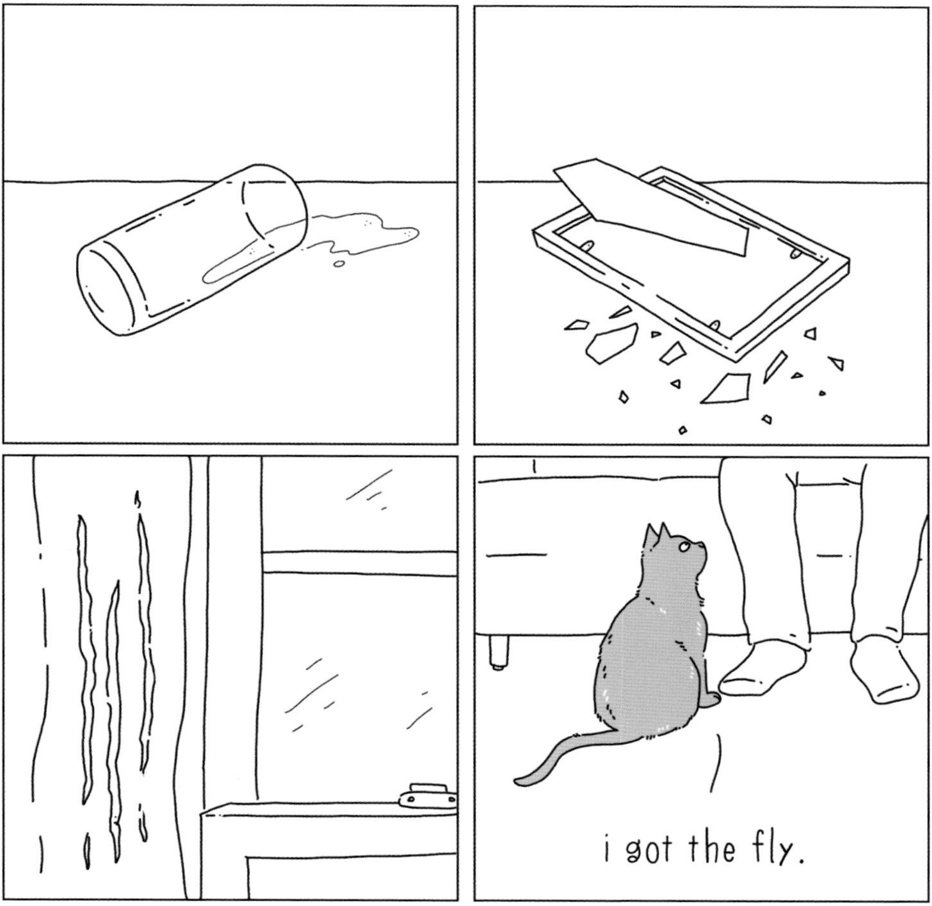
i got the fly.

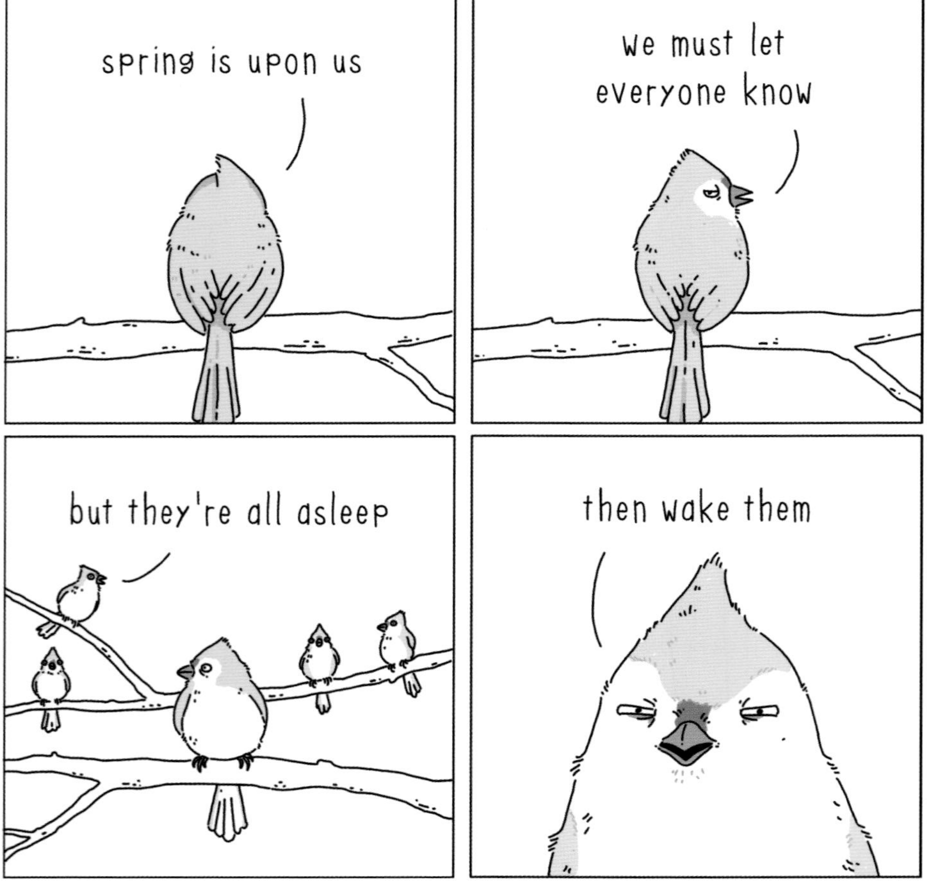
spring is upon us
we must let everyone know
but they're all asleep
then wake them

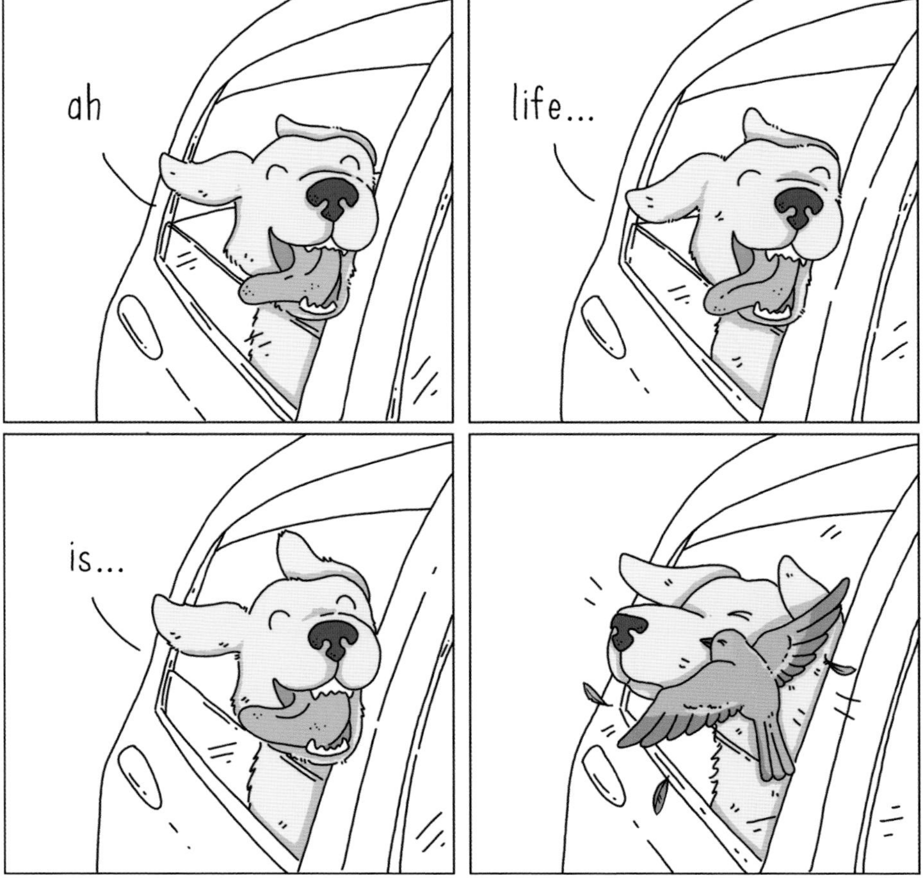
ah
life...
is...

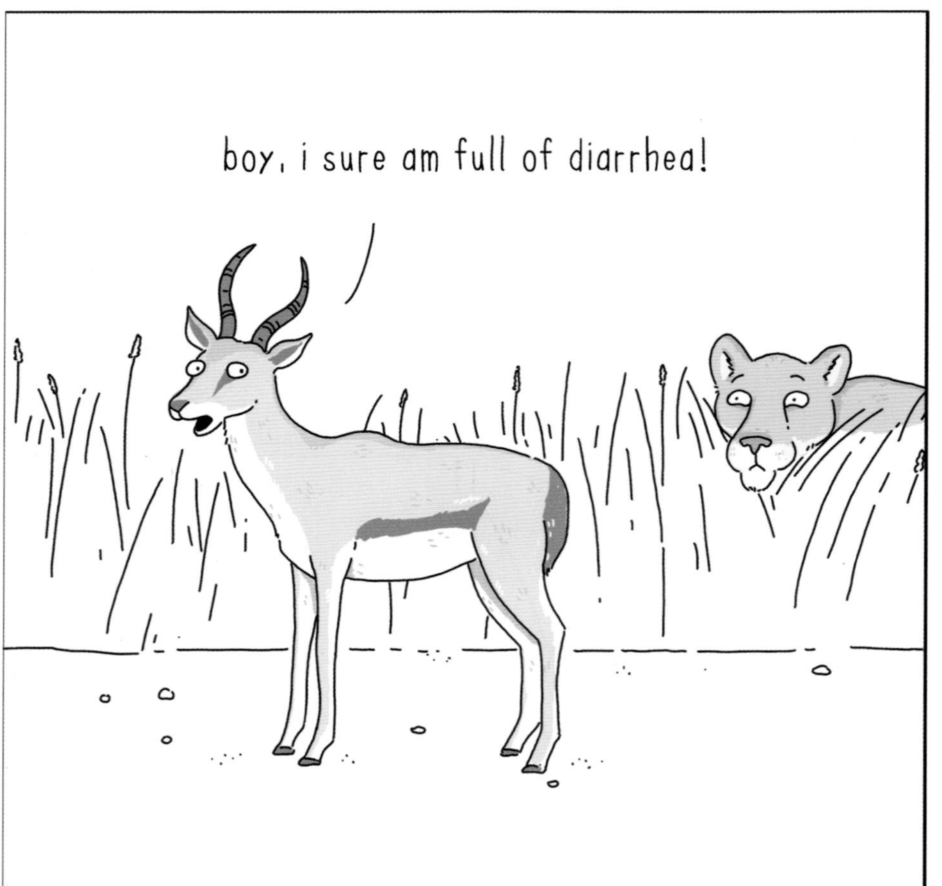
boy, i sure am full of diarrhea!

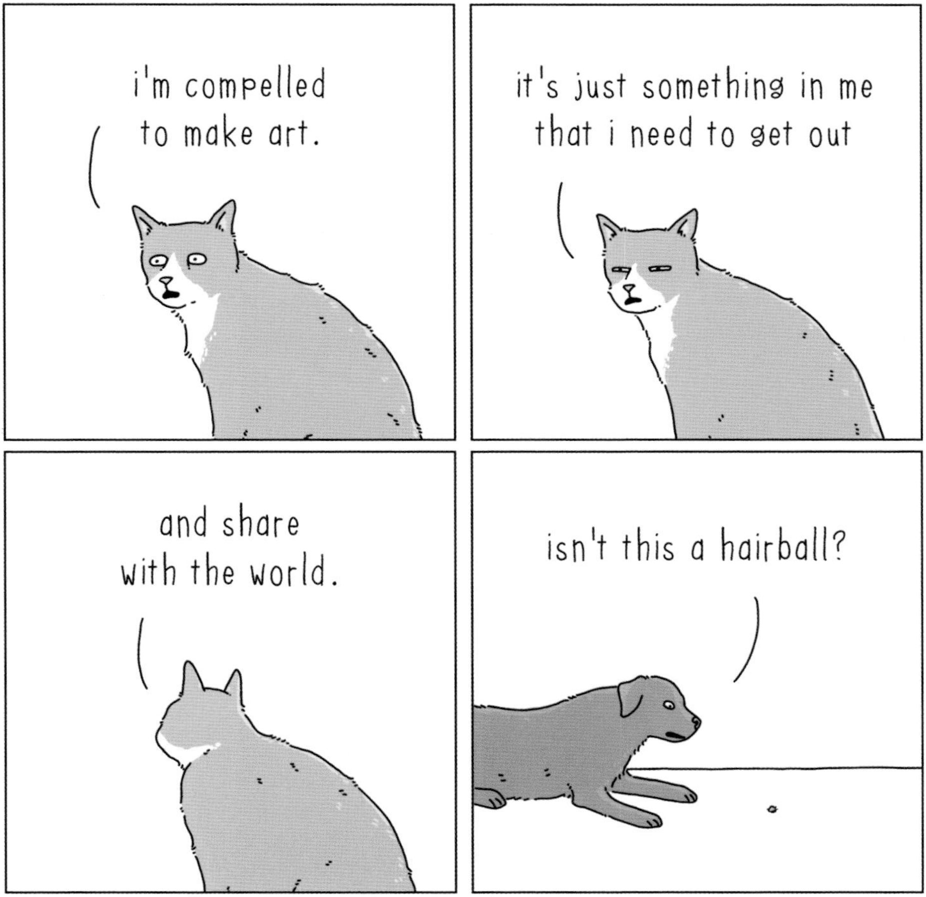
i'm compelled
to make art.
it's just something in me
that i need to get out
and share
with the world.
isn't this a hairball?

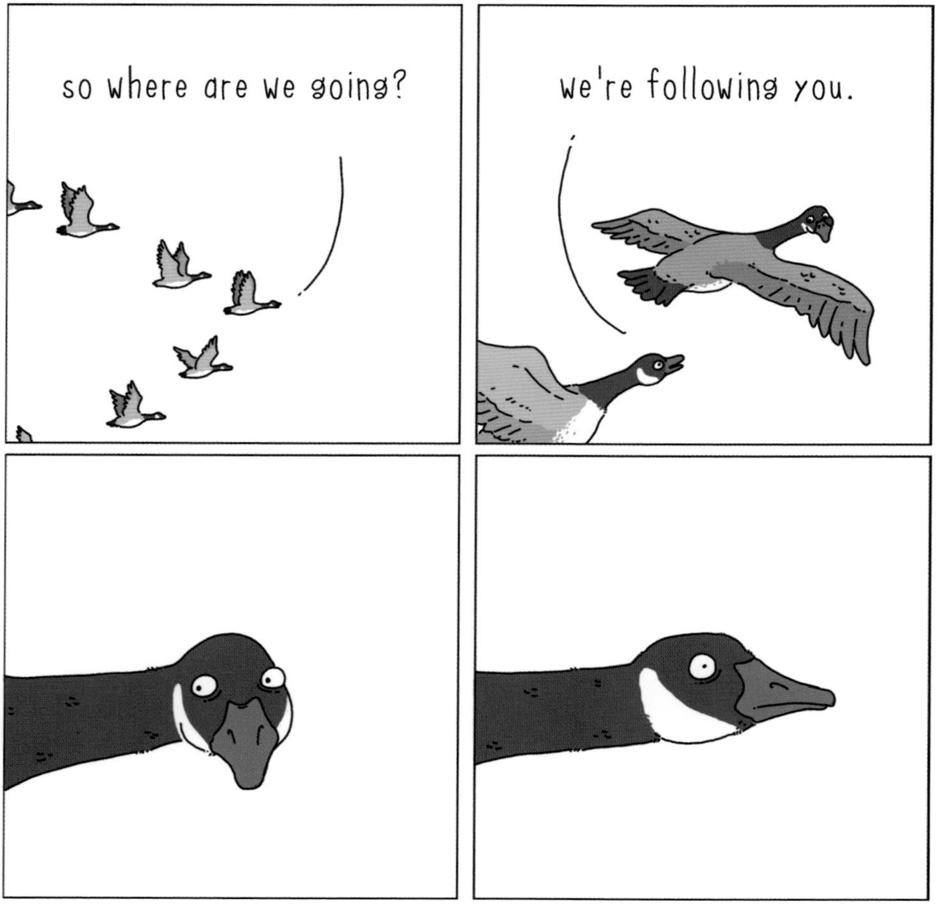
so where are we going?
we're following you.

are we
there yet?

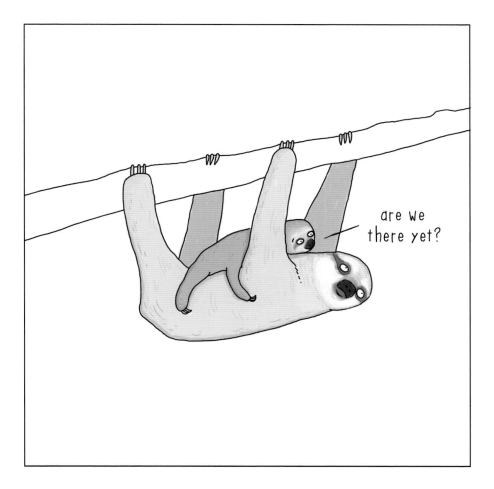

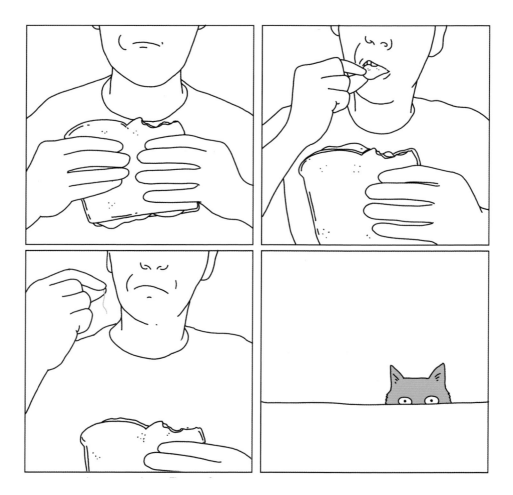

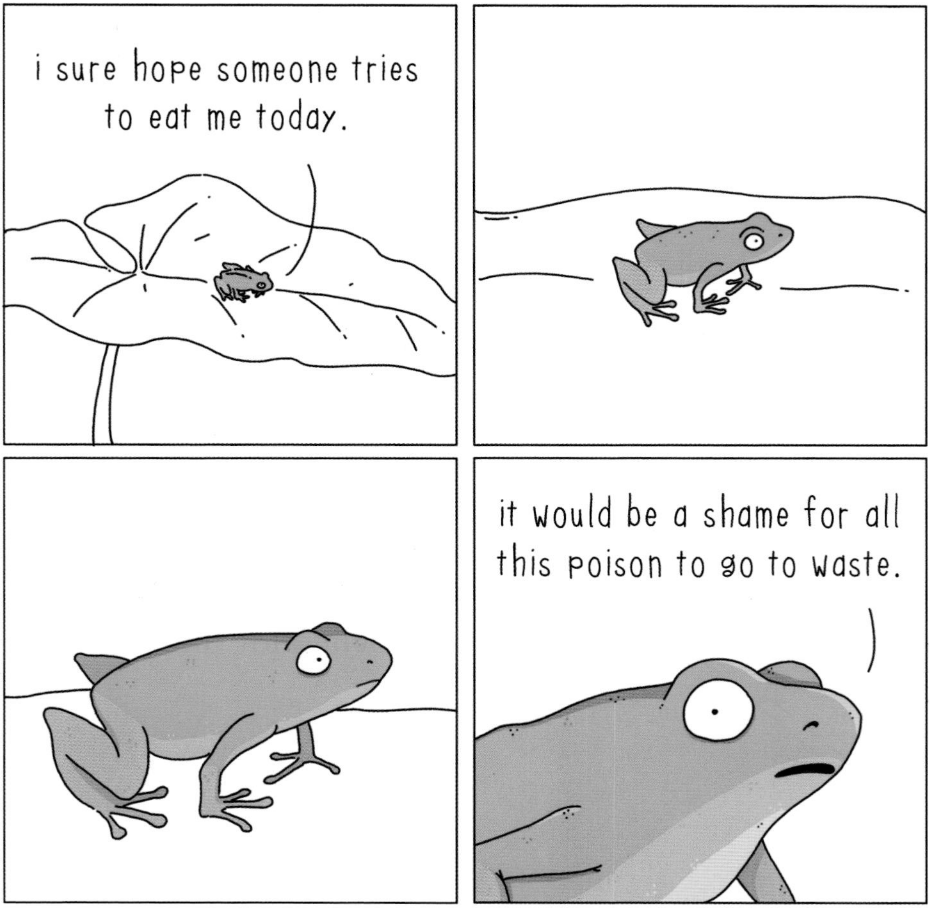
i sure hope someone tries to eat me today.
it would be a shame for all this poison to go to waste.

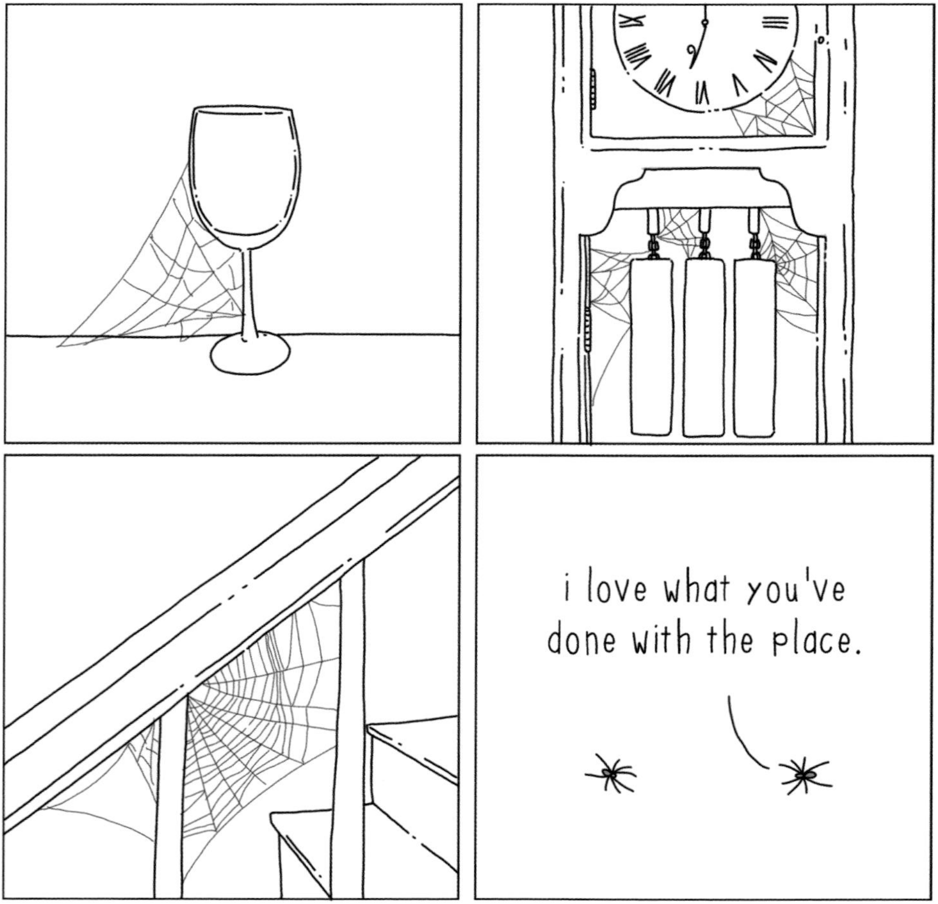
i love what you've
done with the place.

you might want to bring two bags.

oh great, here comes my ex.

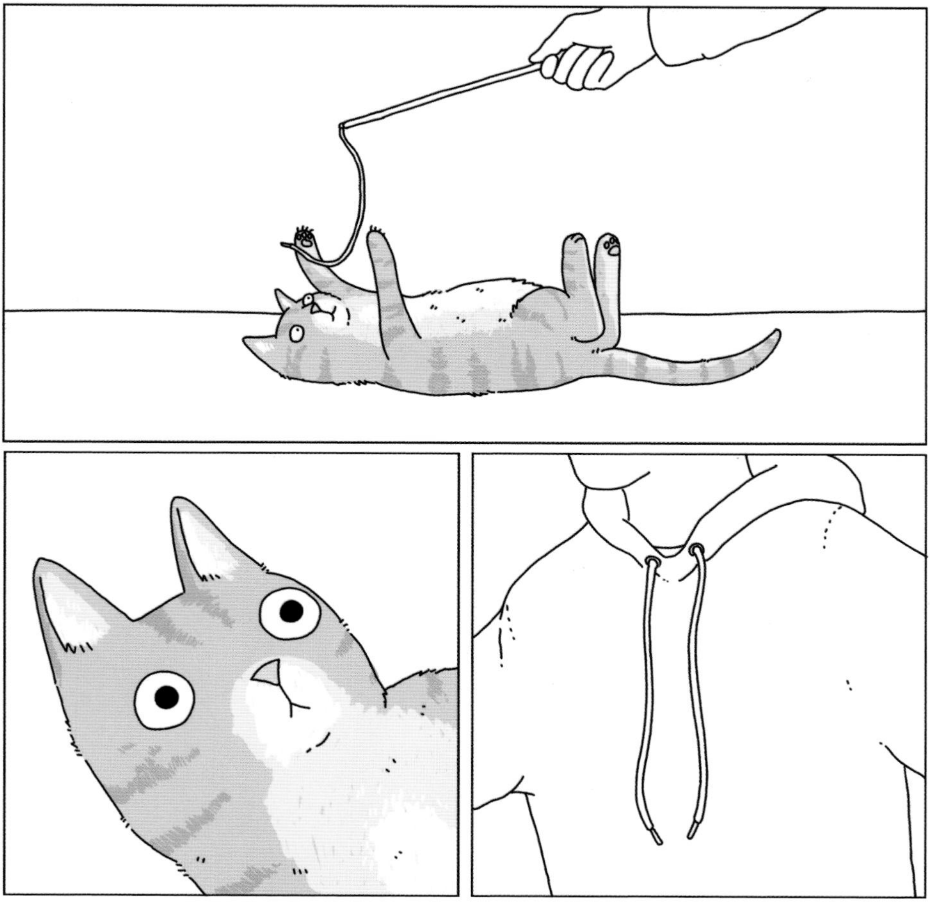

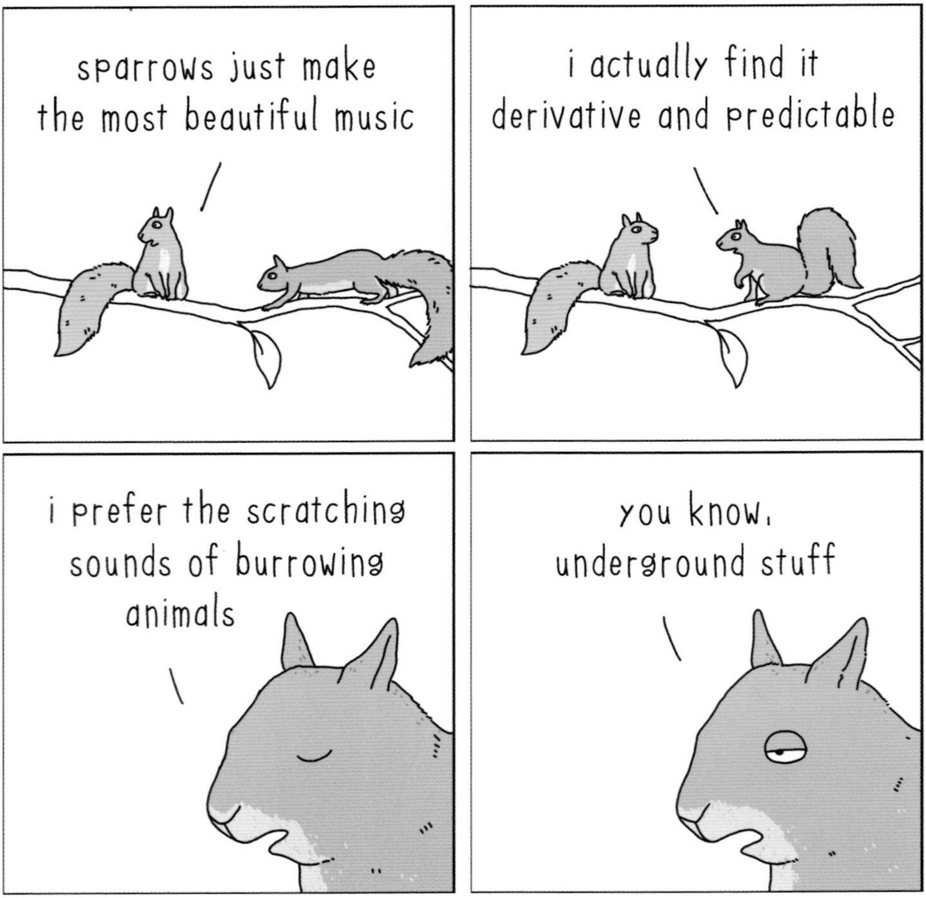
sparrows just make the most beautiful music
i actually find it derivative and predictable
i prefer the scratching sounds of burrowing animals
you know, underground stuff

i've heard so much about cheese, but i've
never met anyone that's actually tried it.

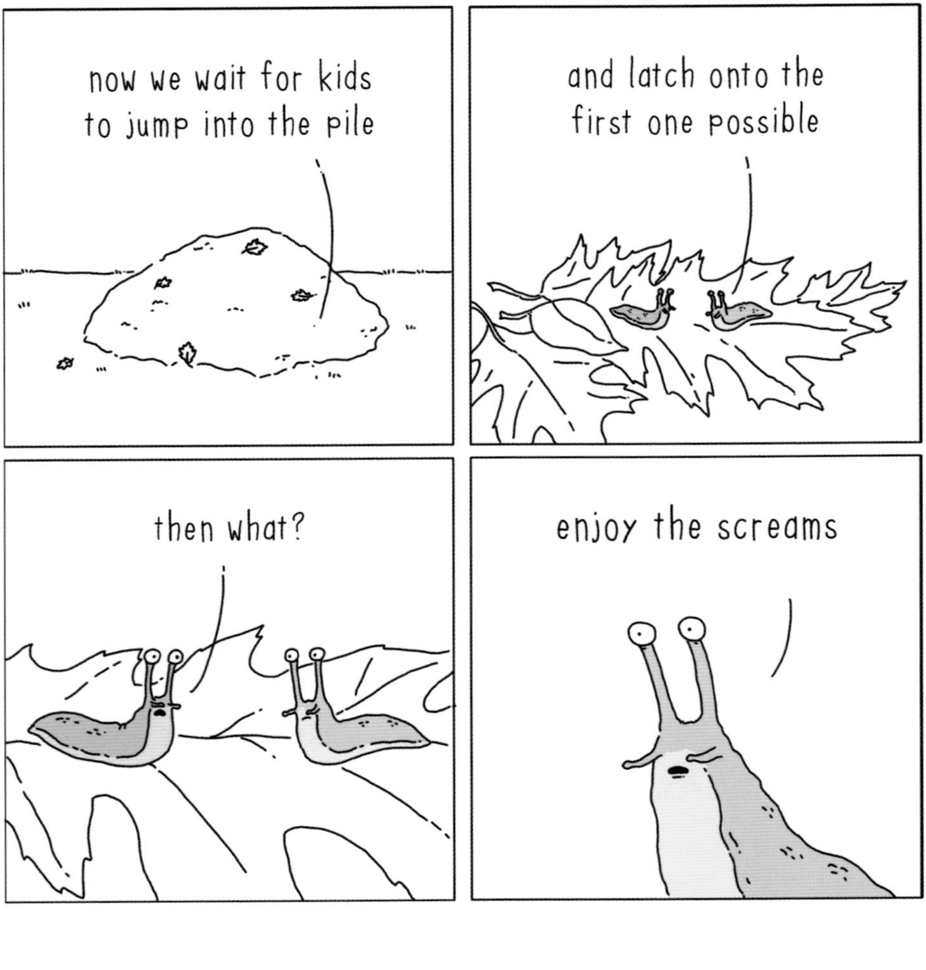
now we wait for kids to jump into the pile
and latch onto the first one possible
then what?
enjoy the screams

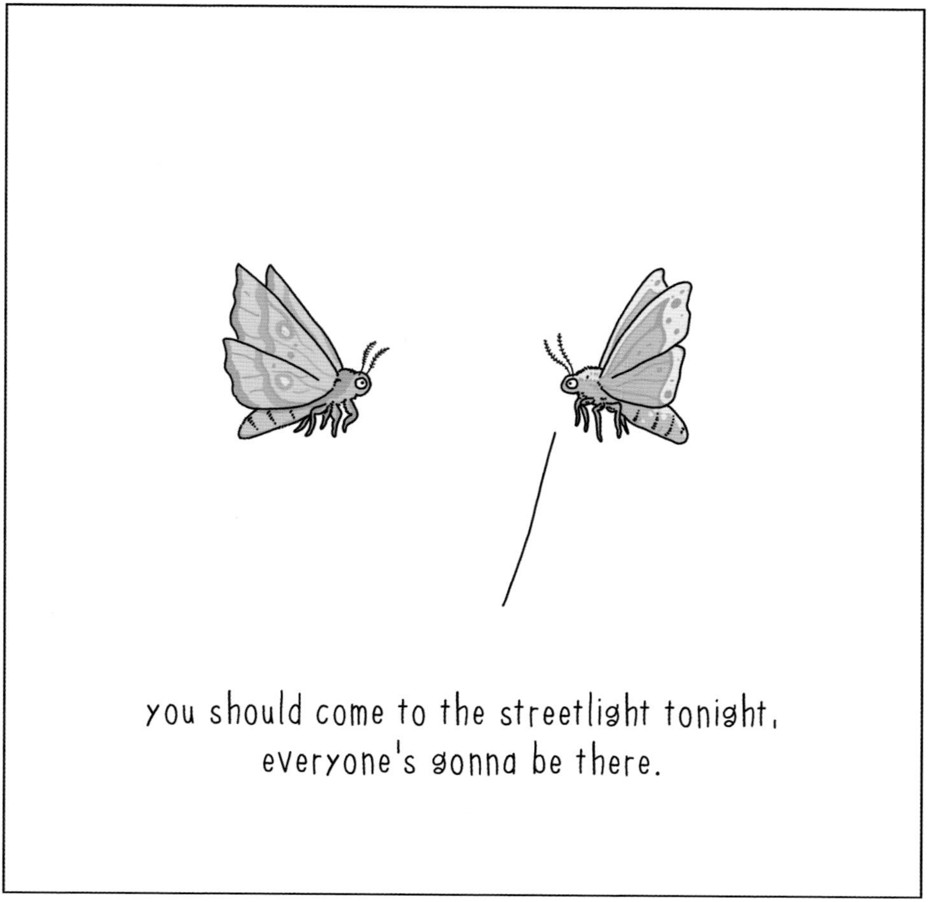
you should come to the streetlight tonight,
everyone's gonna be there.

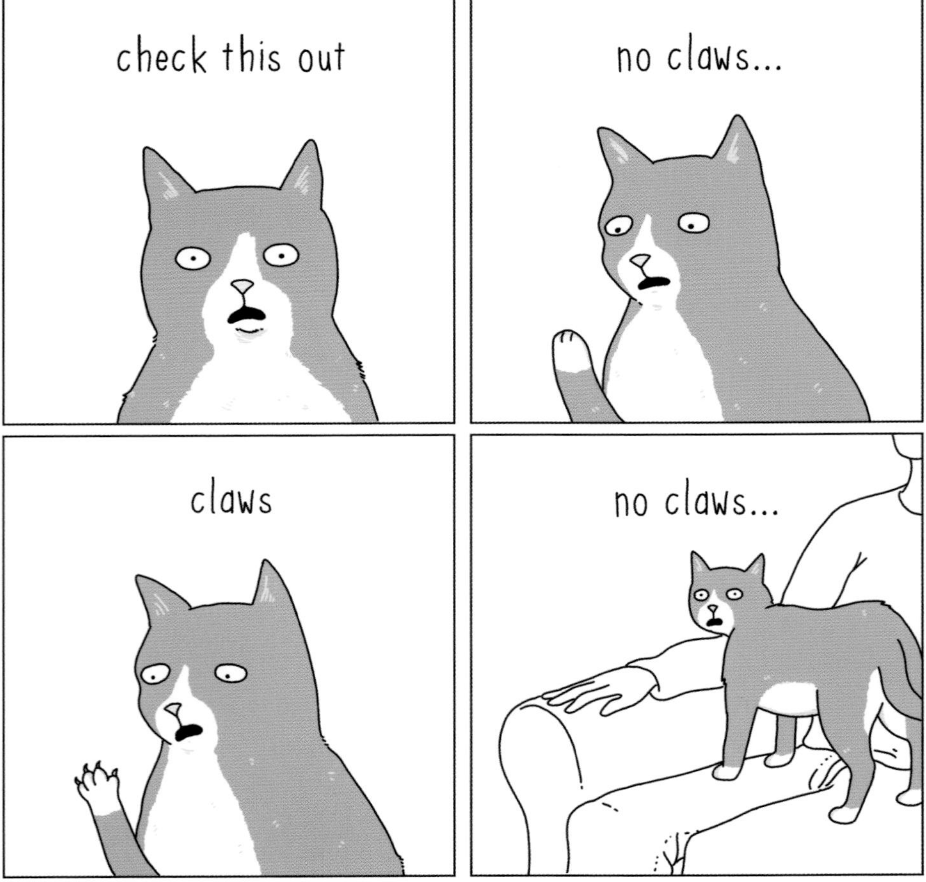
check this out
no claws...
claws
no claws...

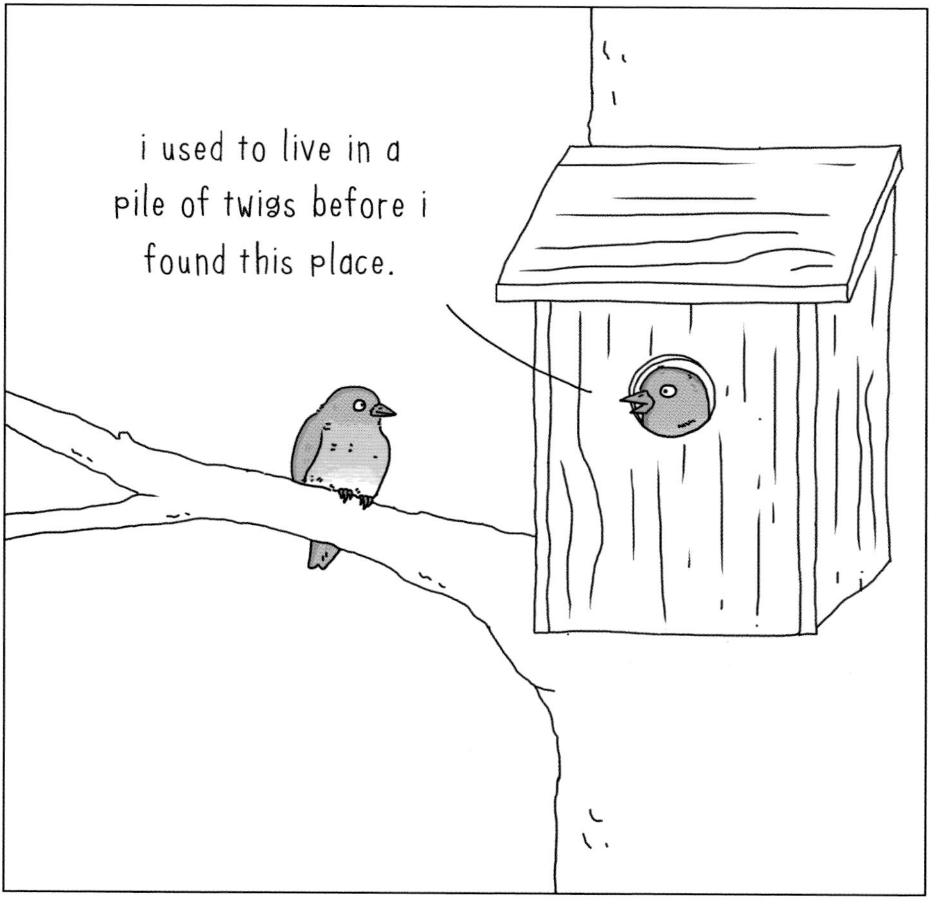
i used to live in a pile of twigs before i found this place.

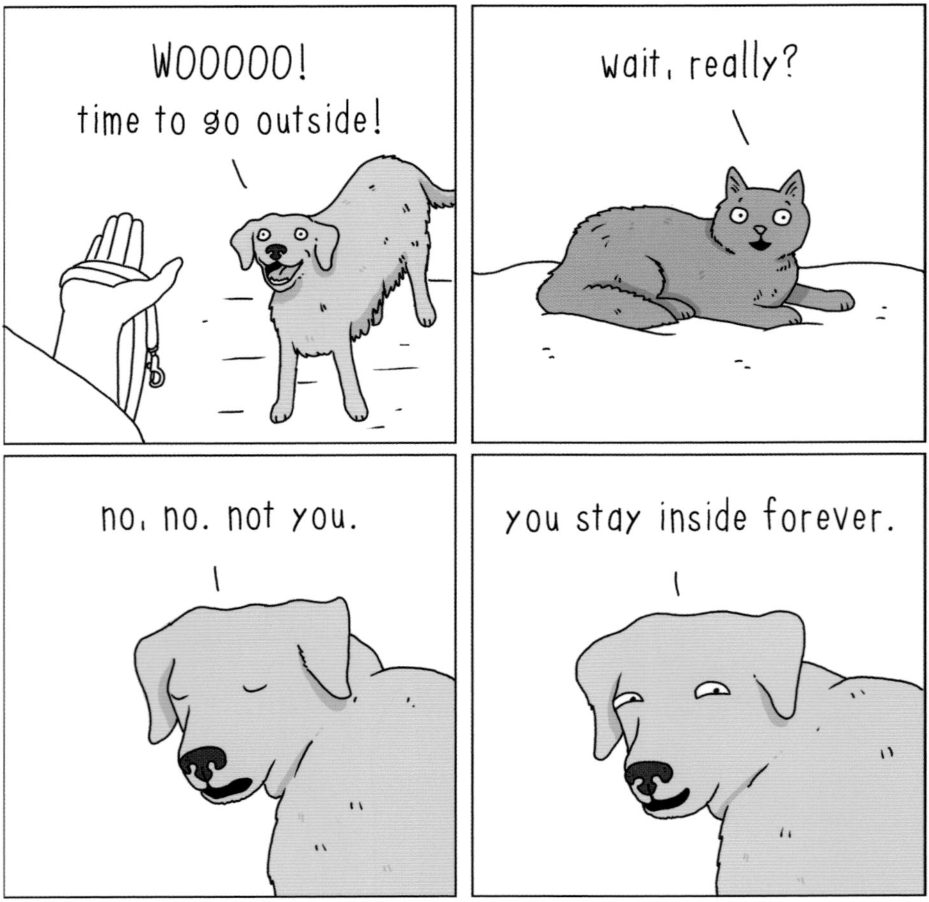
WOOOOO!
time to go outside!
wait, really?
no, no. not you.
you stay inside forever.

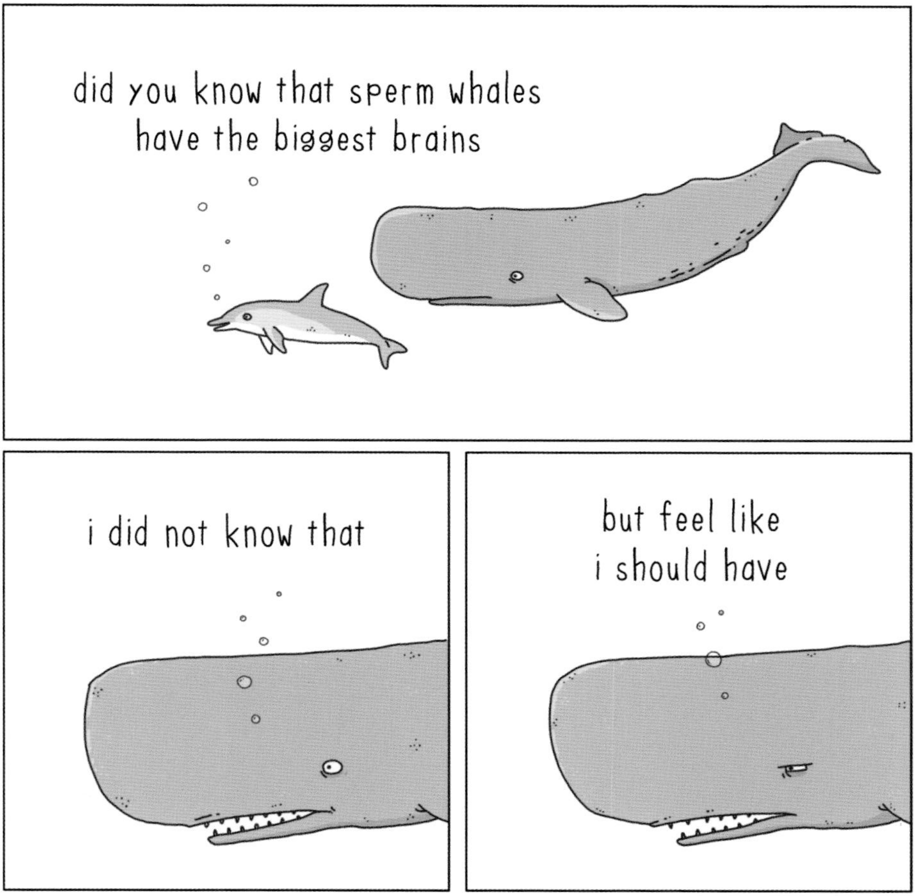
did you know that sperm whales
have the biggest brains
i did not know that
but feel like
i should have

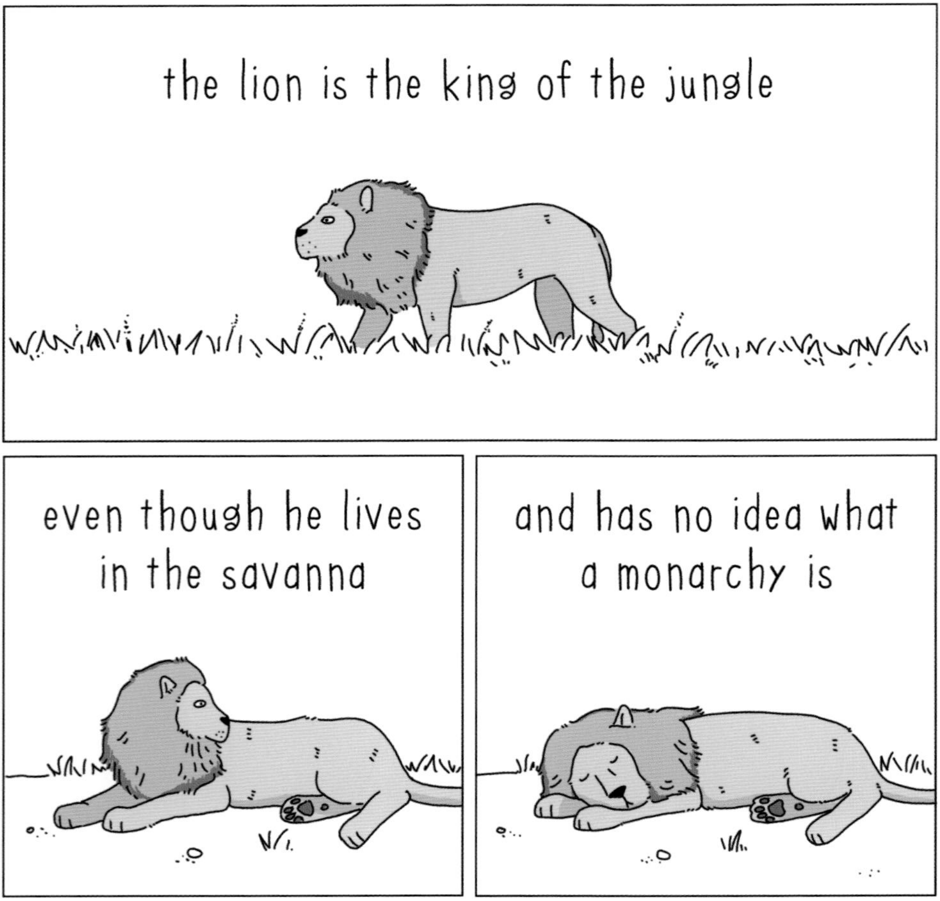
the lion is the king of the jungle
even though he lives in the savanna
and has no idea what a monarchy is

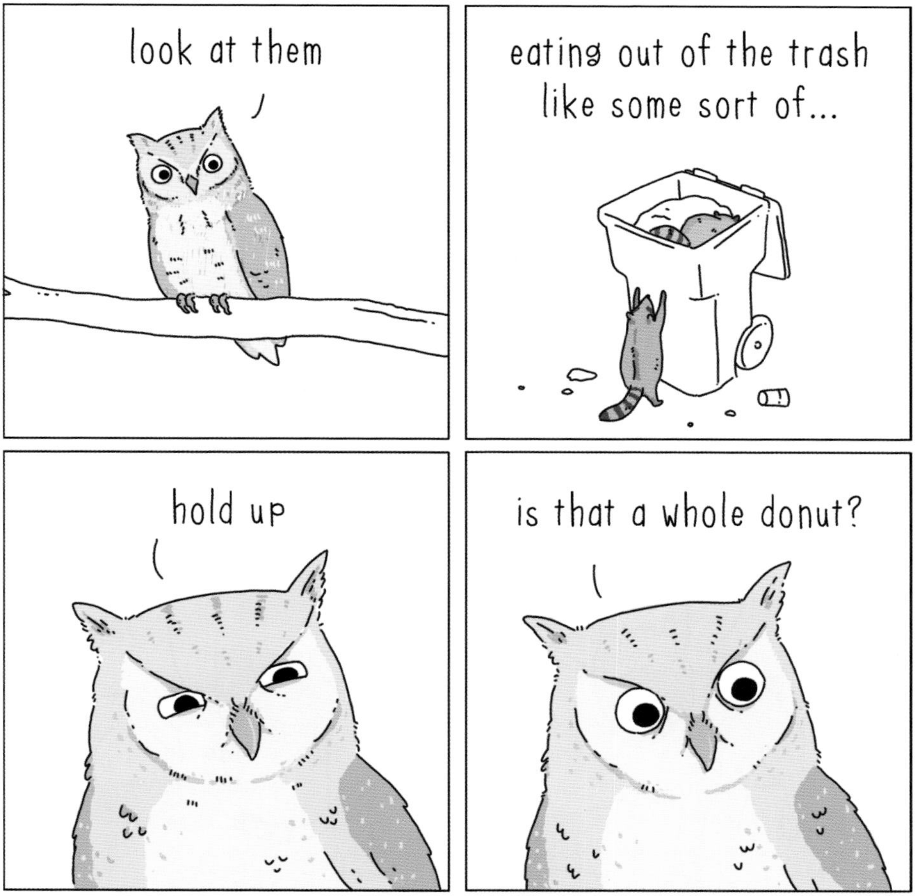
look at them
eating out of the trash like some sort of...
hold up
is that a whole donut?

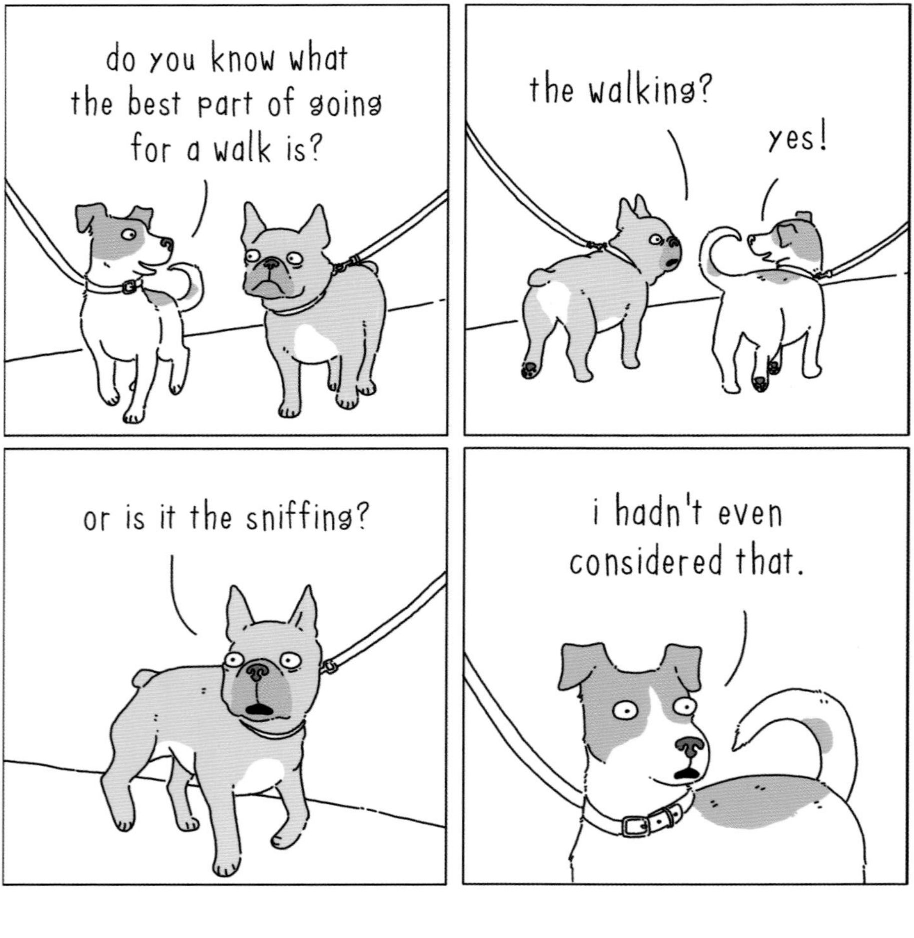
do you know what the best part of going for a walk is?
the walking?
yes!
or is it the sniffing?
i hadn't even considered that.

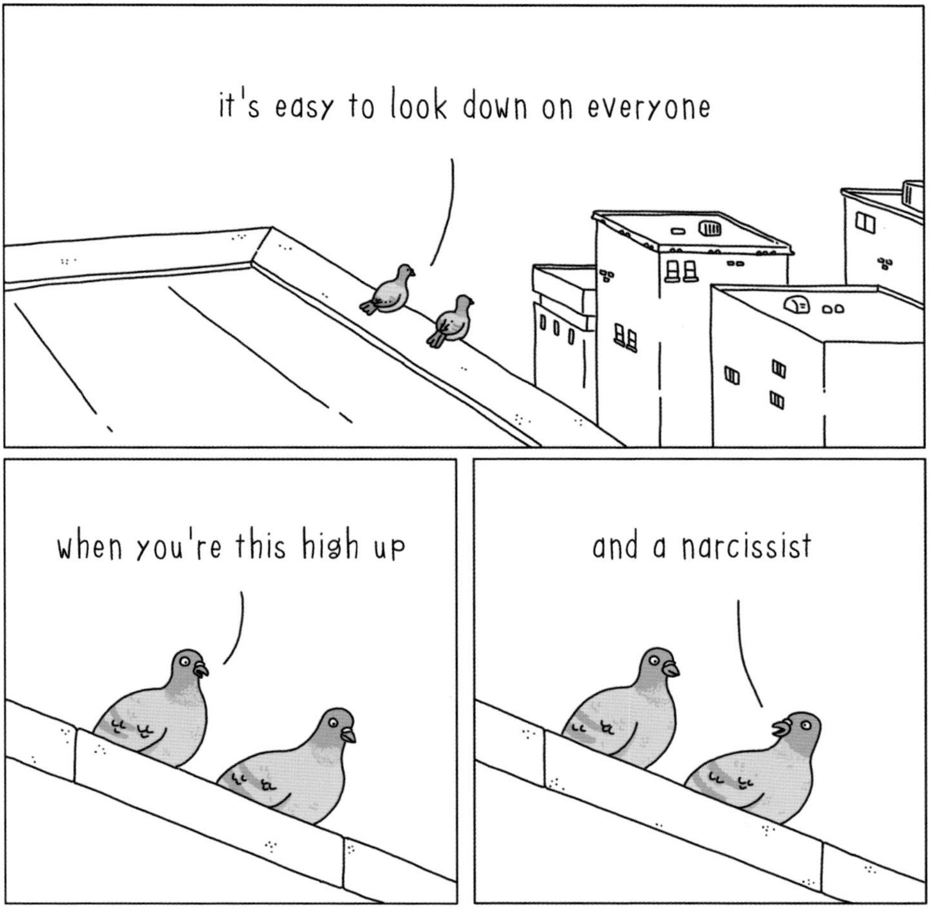
it's easy to look down on everyone
when you're this high up
and a narcissist

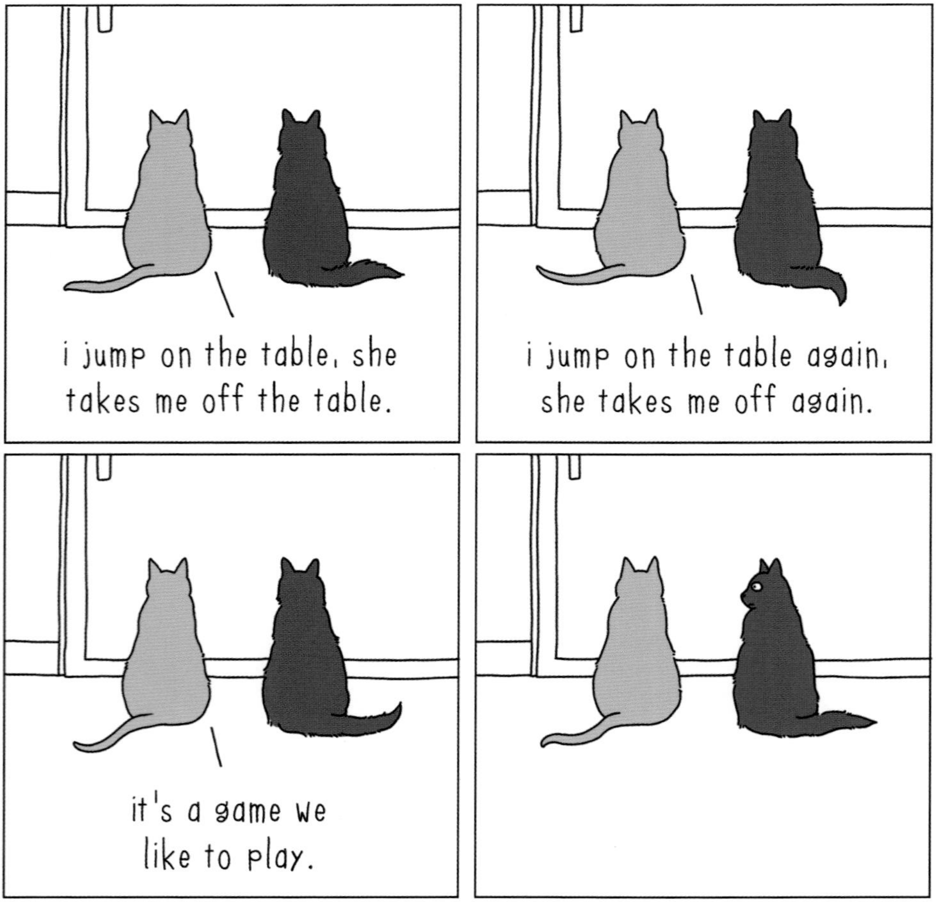
i jump on the table, she takes me off the table.
i jump on the table again, she takes me off again.
it's a game we like to play.

this must be where sticks are made.

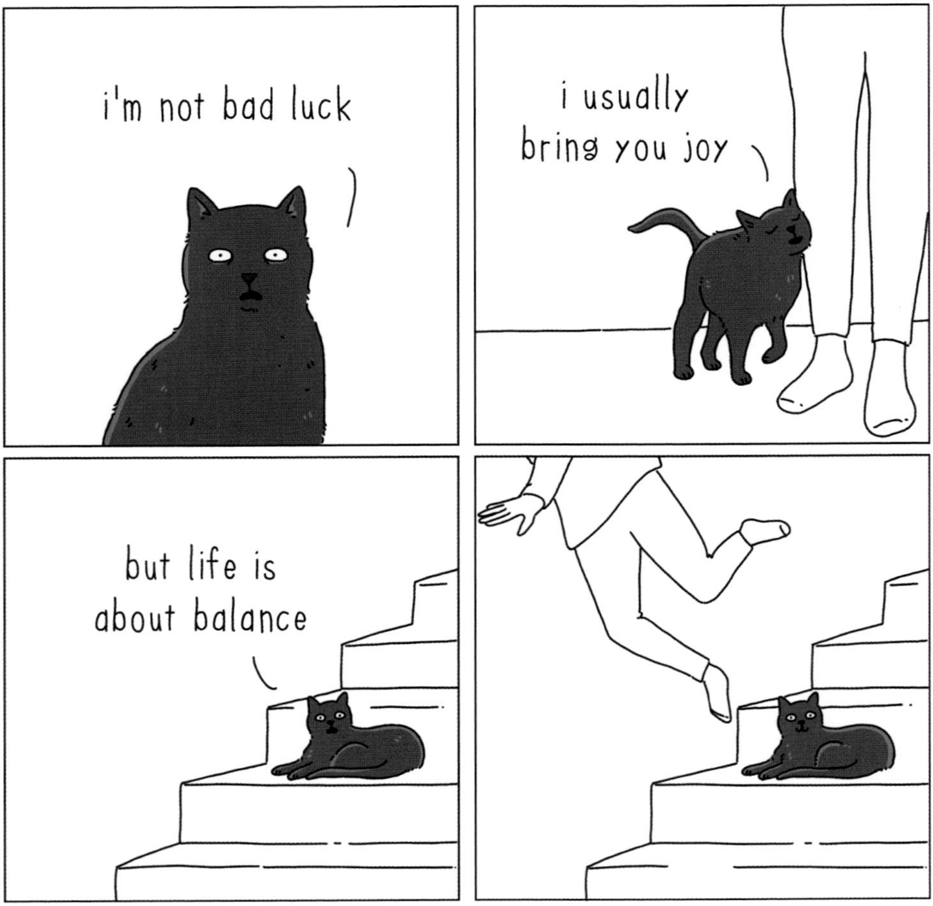
i'm not bad luck
i usually bring you joy
but life is about balance

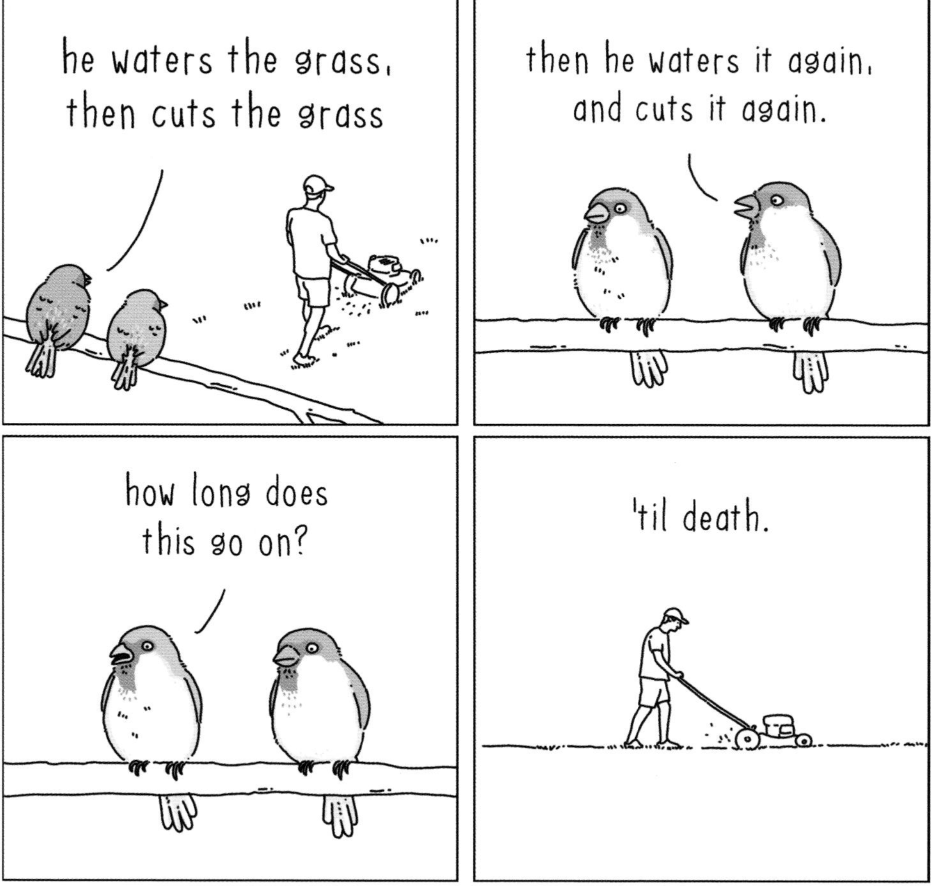
he waters the grass, then cuts the grass
then he waters it again, and cuts it again.
how long does this go on?
'til death.

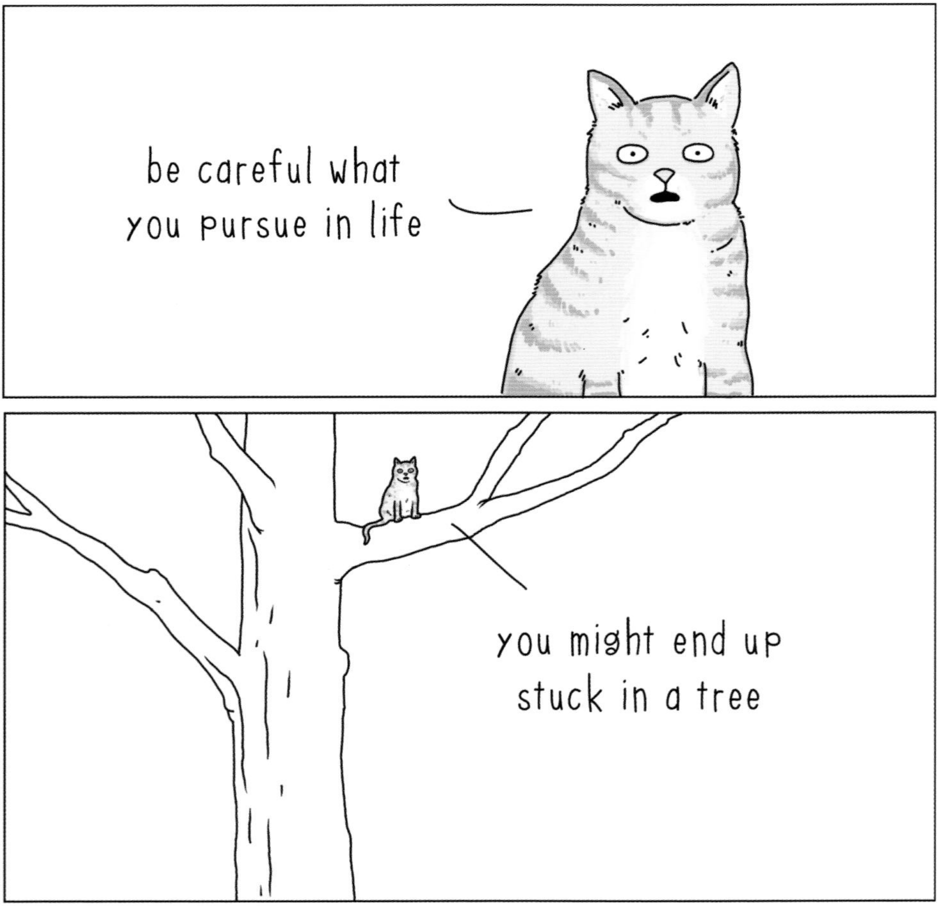
be careful what
you pursue in life
you might end up
stuck in a tree

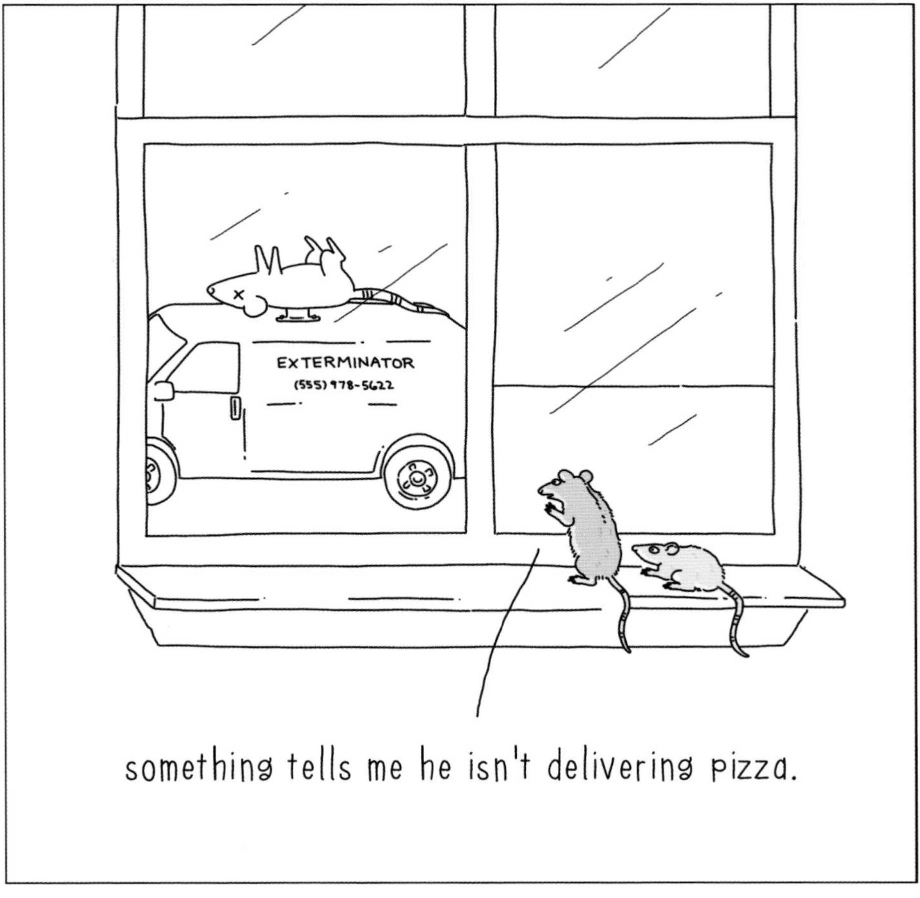
EXTERMINATOR
(555) 978-5622

something tells me he isn't delivering pizza.

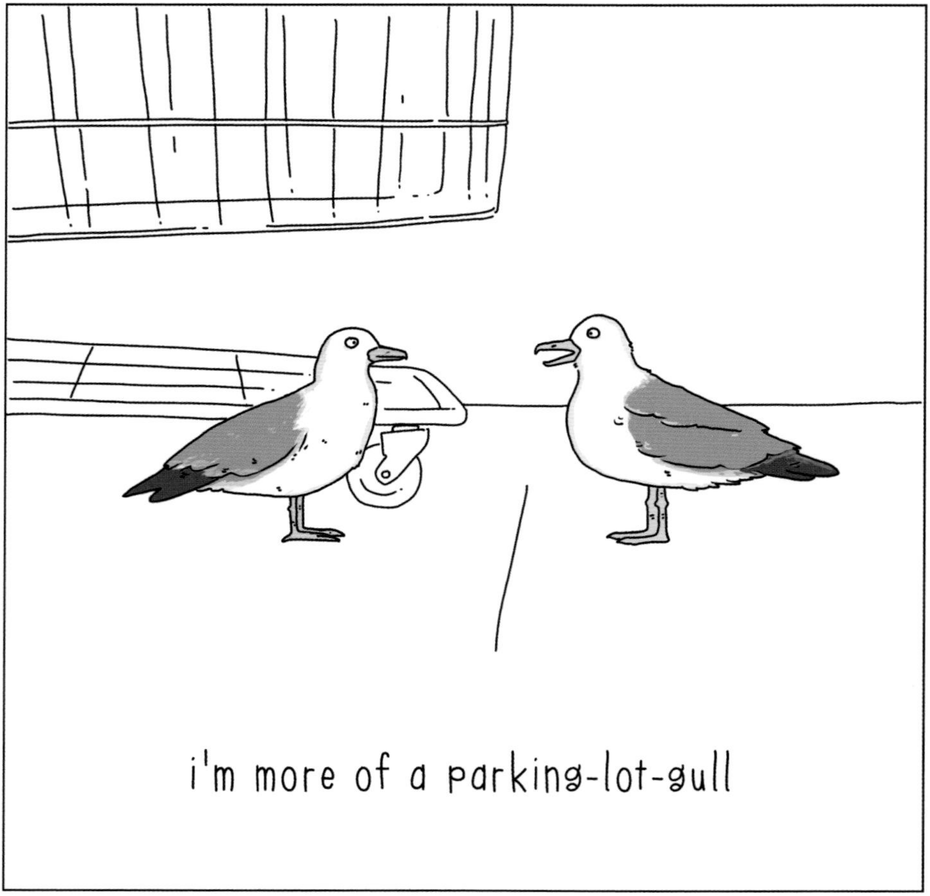
i'm more of a parking-lot-gull

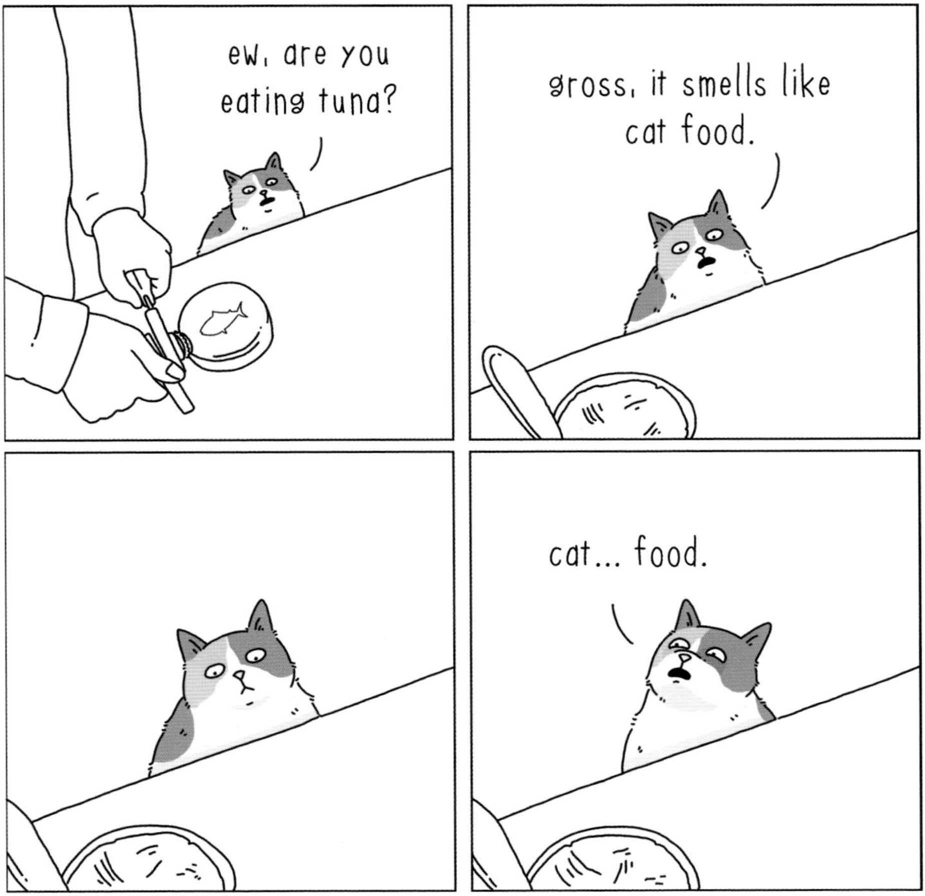
ew, are you eating tuna?
gross, it smells like cat food.
cat... food.

why do i have to parade around and put on a show to attract someone?
why can't i just be myself?
well... it depends on who you want to attract.

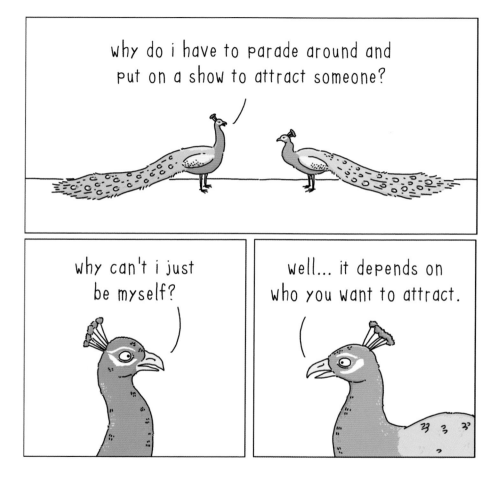

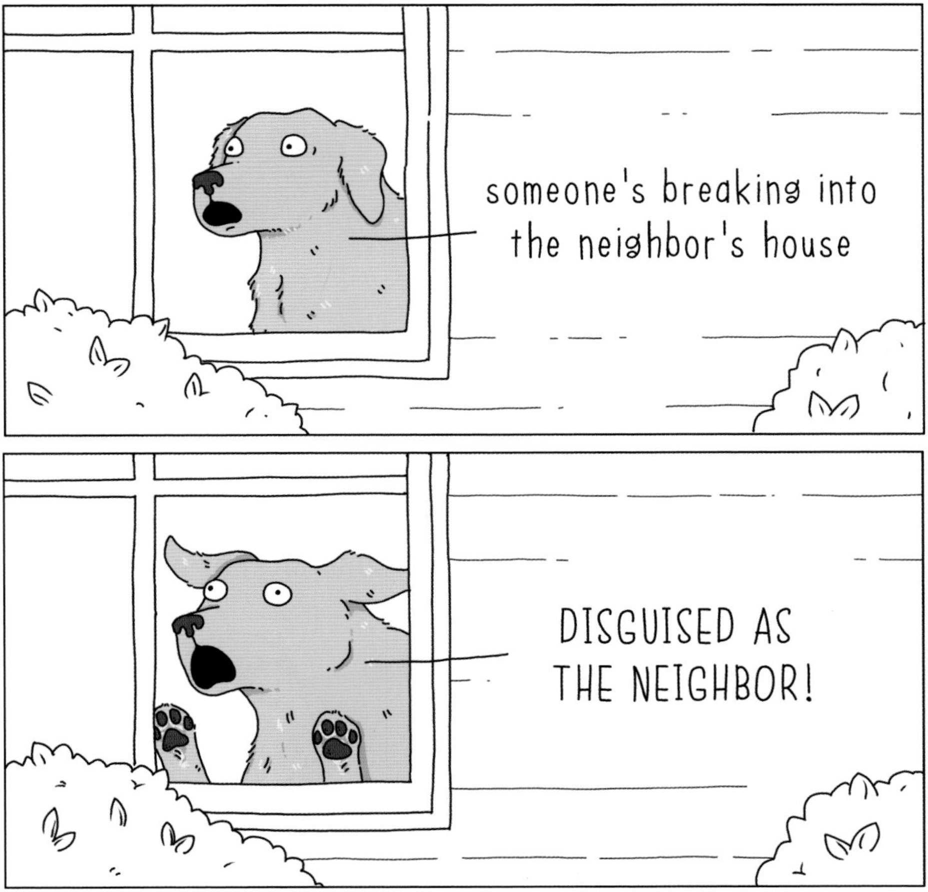
someone's breaking into the neighbor's house
DISGUISED AS THE NEIGHBOR!

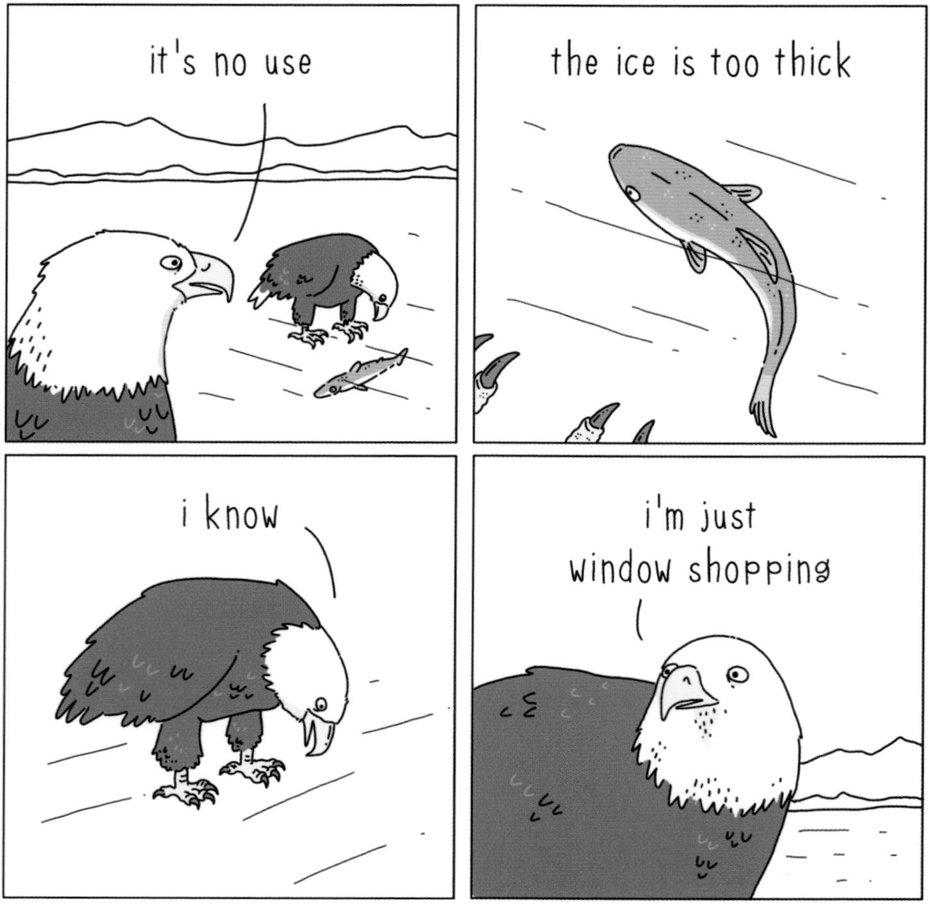
it's no use
the ice is too thick
i know
i'm just
window shopping

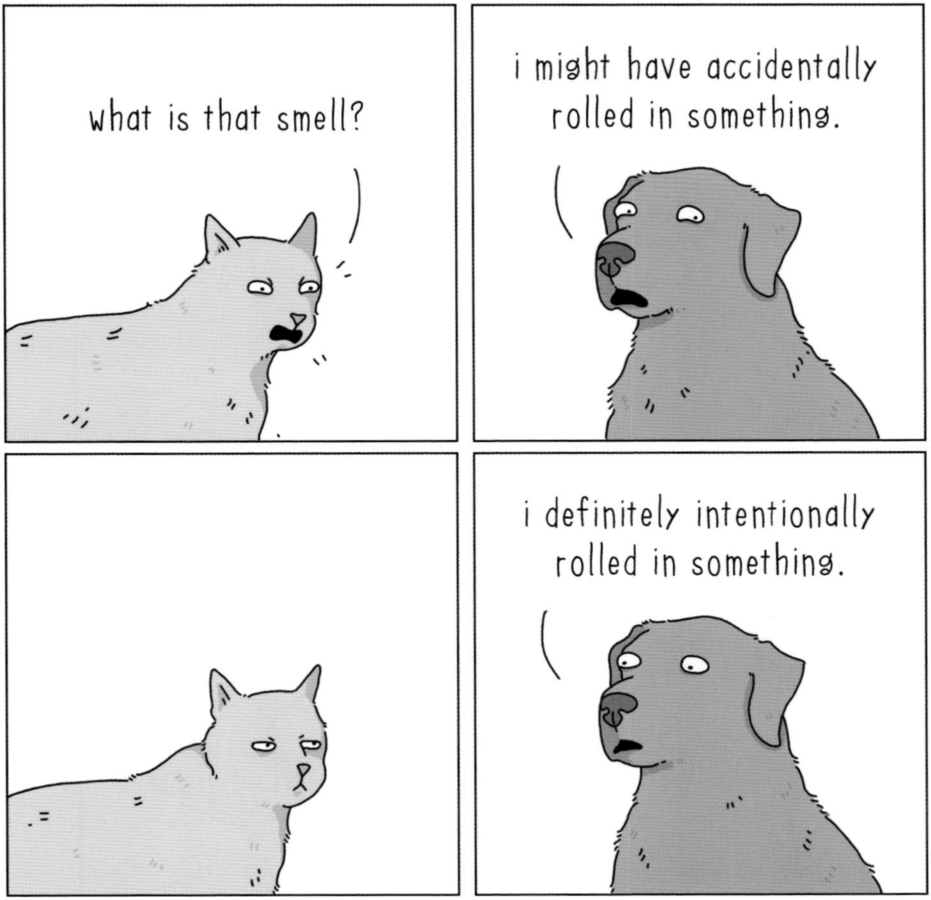
what is that smell?
i might have accidentally rolled in something.
i definitely intentionally rolled in something.

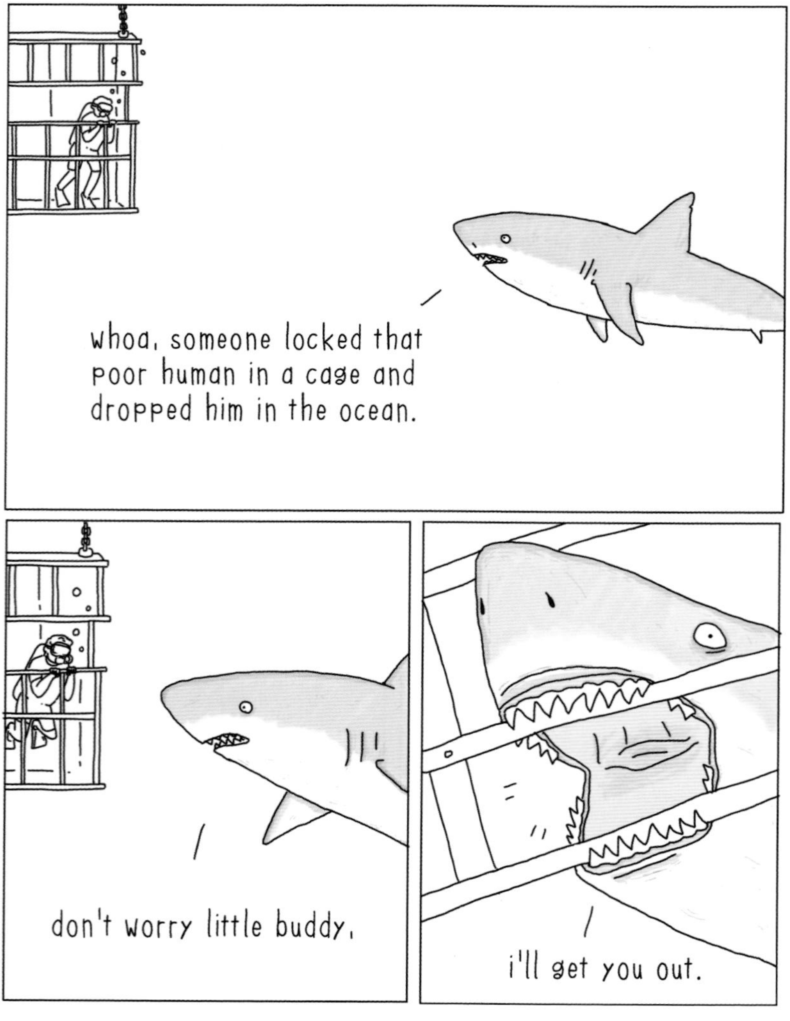
whoa, someone locked that poor human in a cage and dropped him in the ocean.
don't worry little buddy,
i'll get you out.

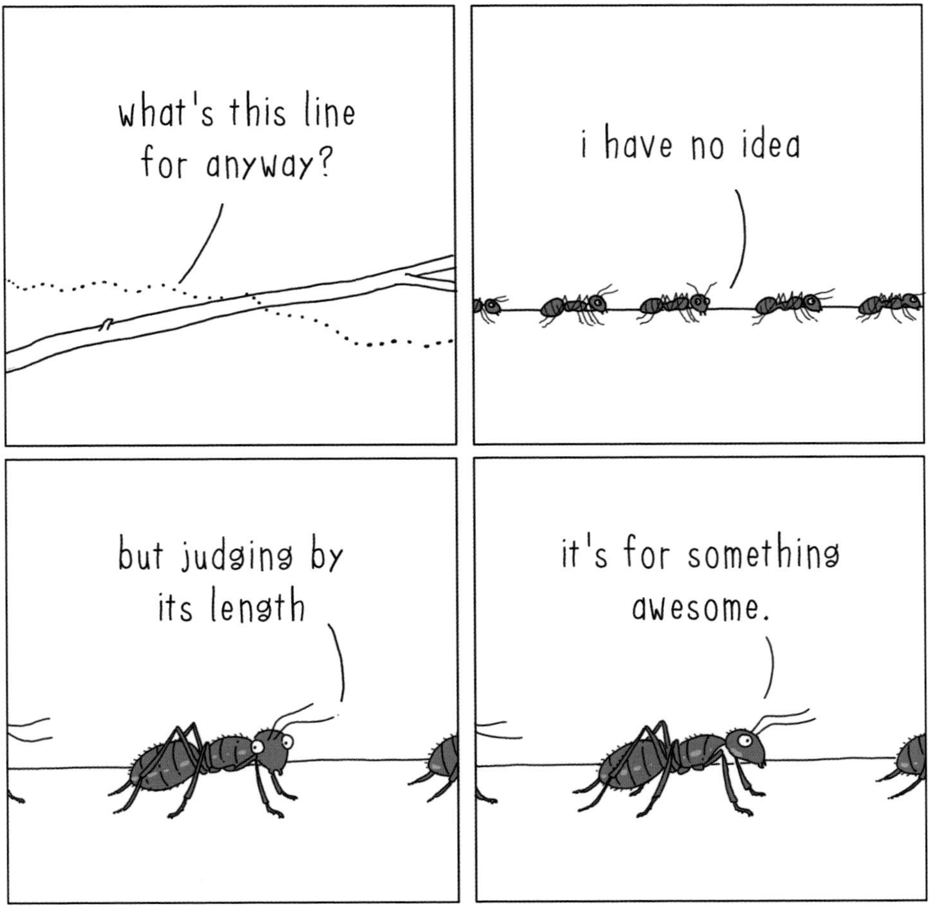
what's this line for anyway?
i have no idea
but judging by its length
it's for something awesome.

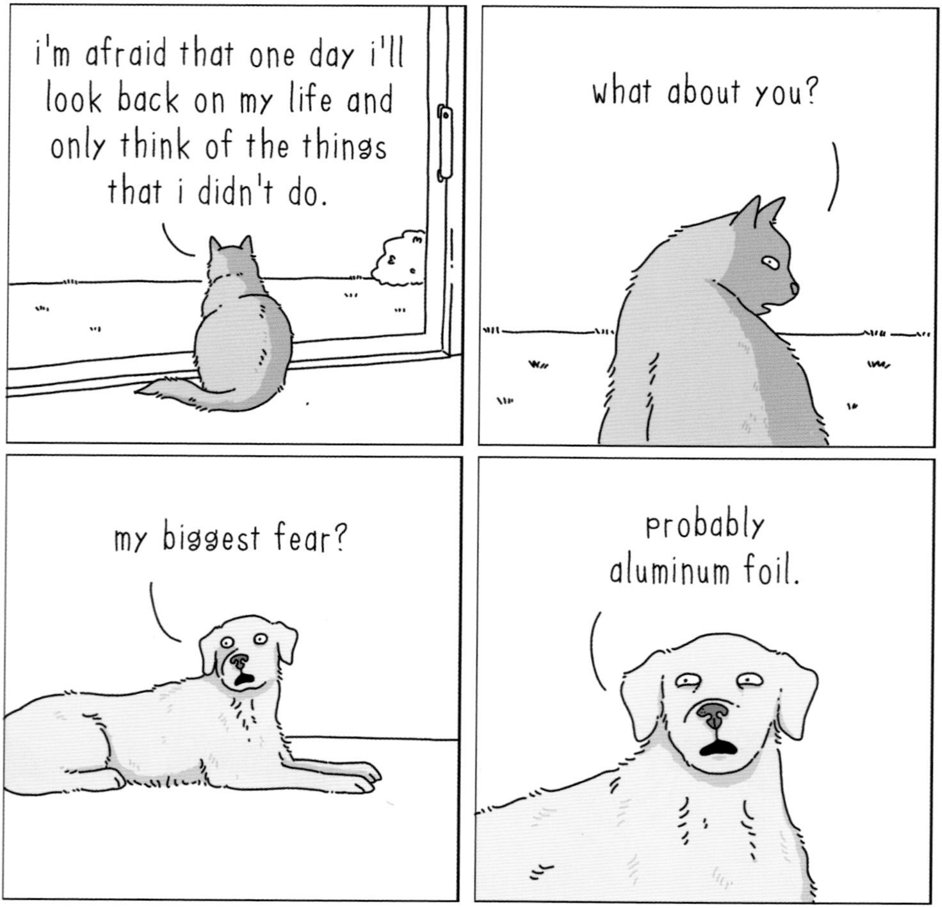
i'm afraid that one day i'll look back on my life and only think of the things that i didn't do.
what about you?
my biggest fear?
probably aluminum foil.

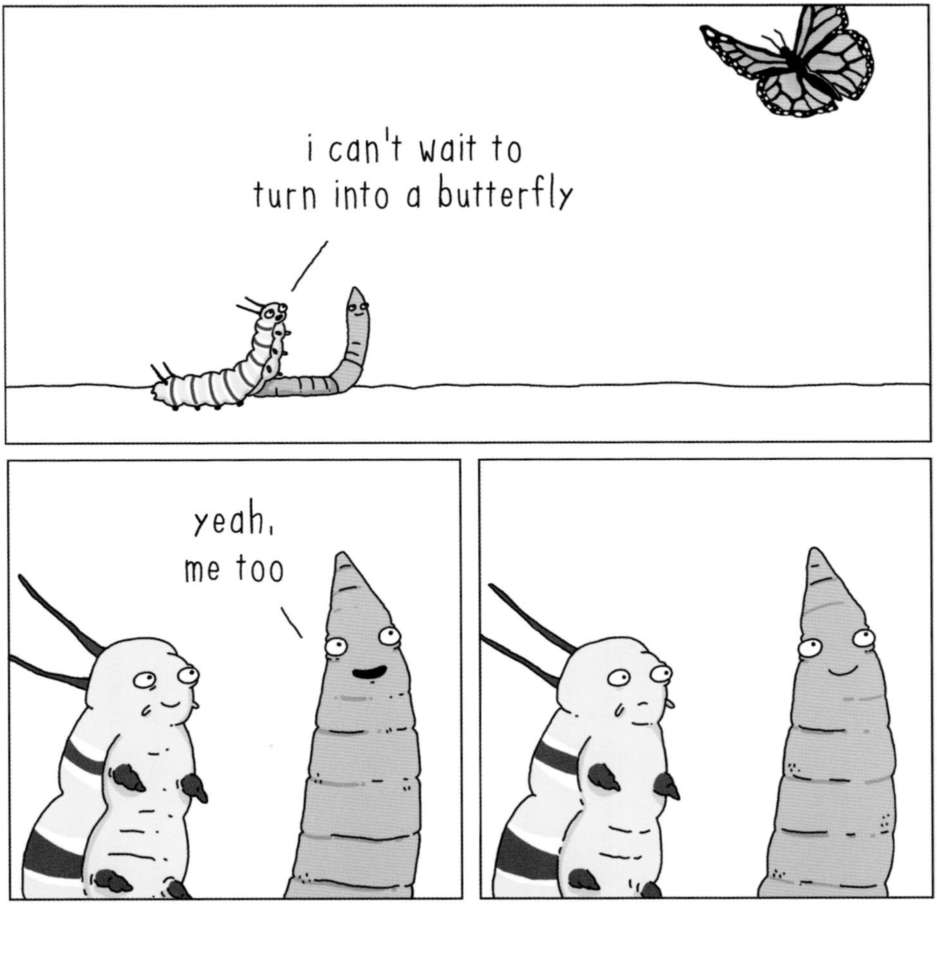
i can't wait to
turn into a butterfly
yeah,
me too

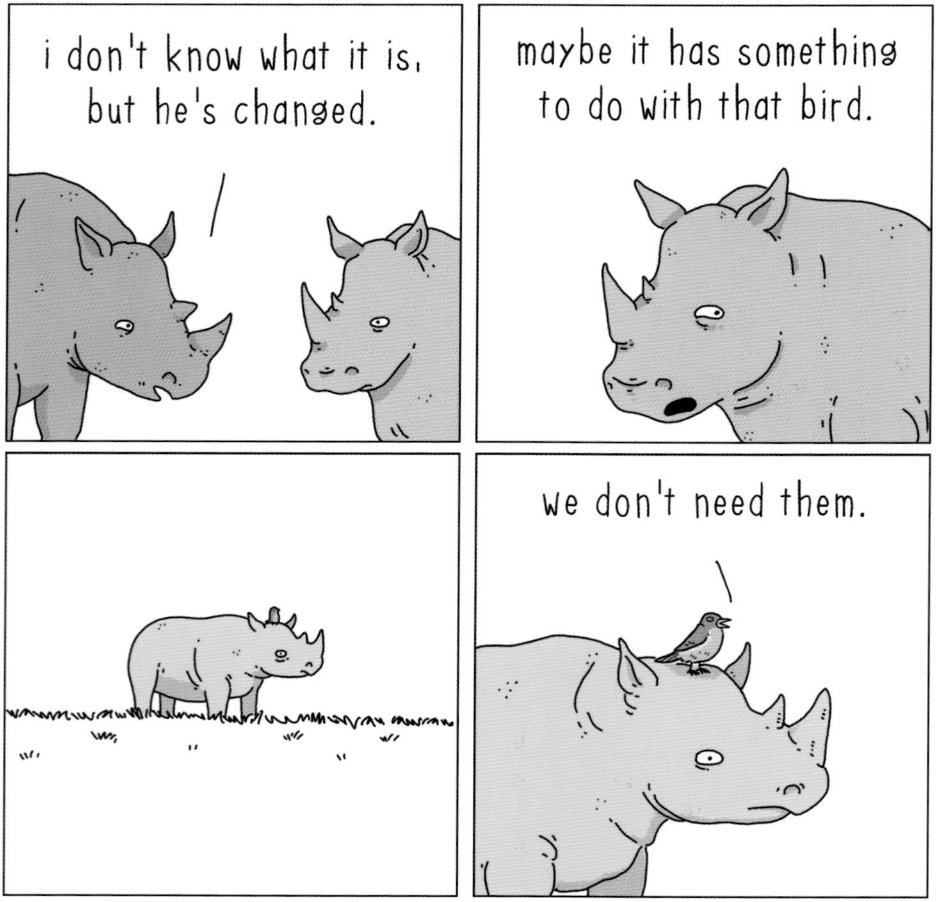
i don't know what it is, but he's changed.
maybe it has something to do with that bird.
we don't need them.

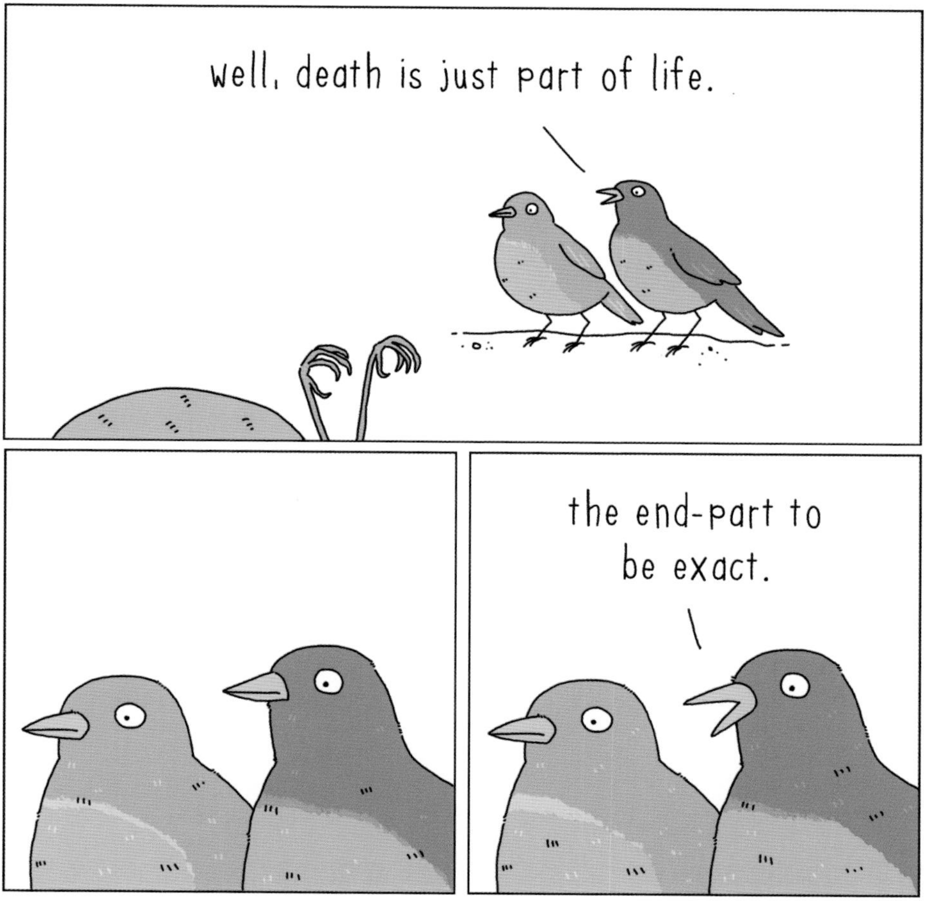
well, death is just part of life.
the end-part to be exact.

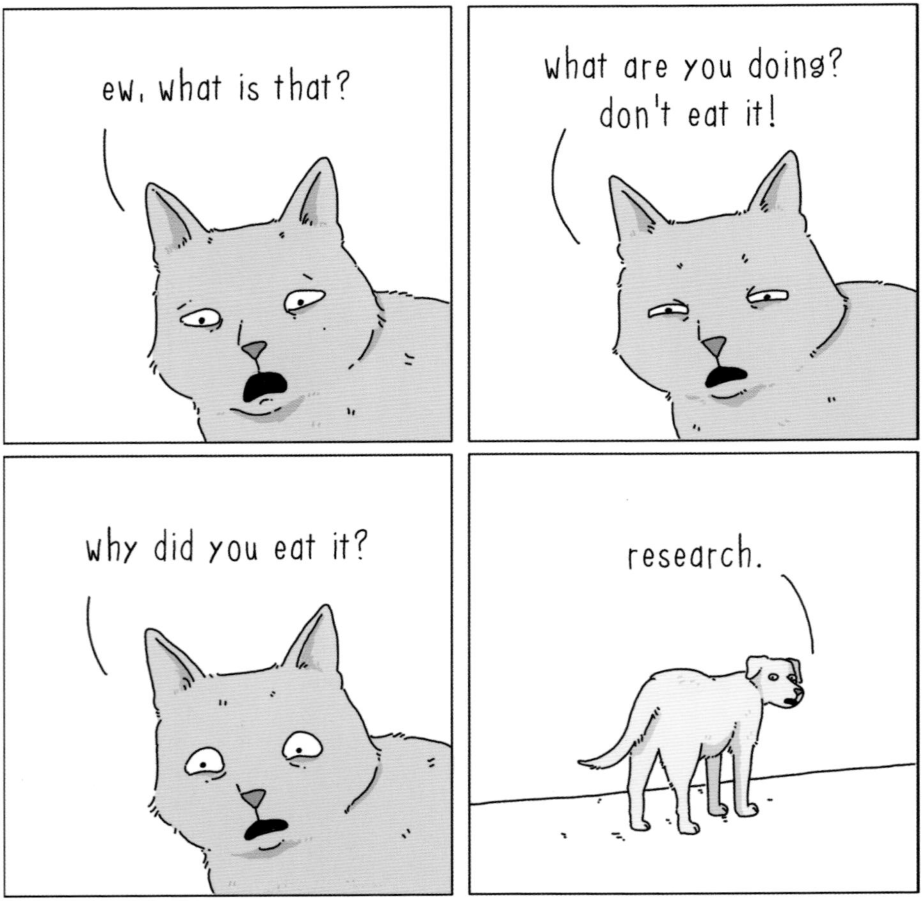
ew, what is that?
what are you doing? don't eat it!
why did you eat it?
research.

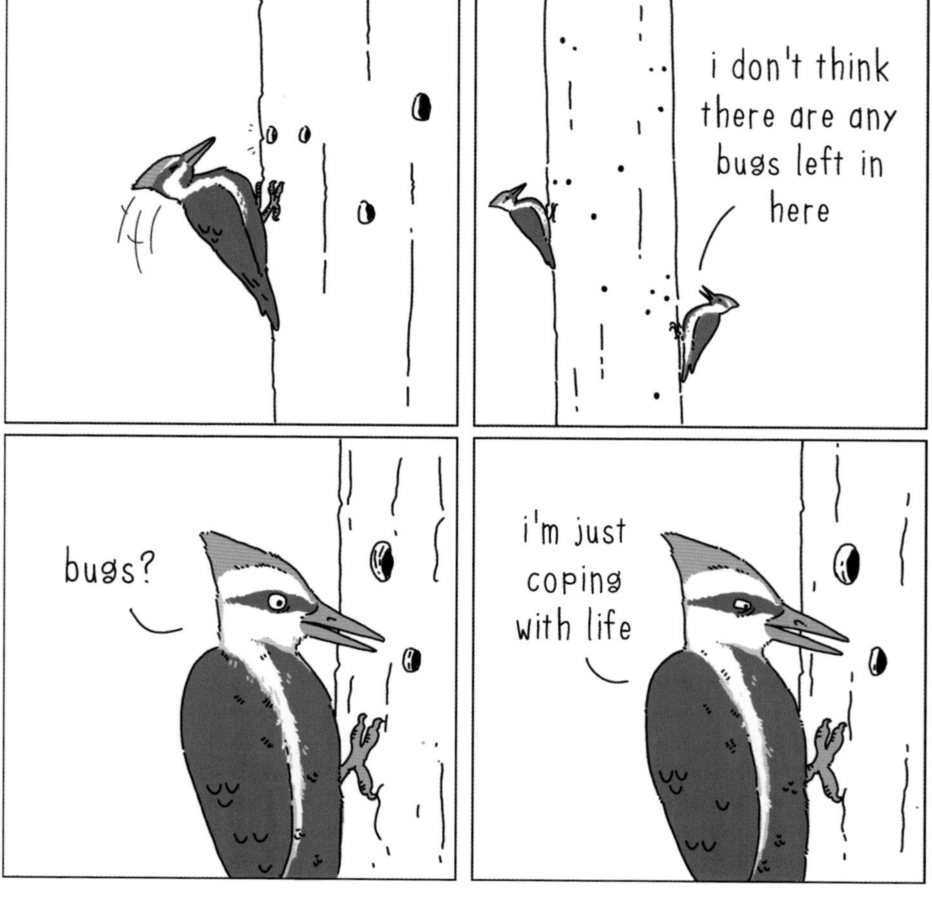
i don't think there are any bugs left in here
bugs?
i'm just coping with life

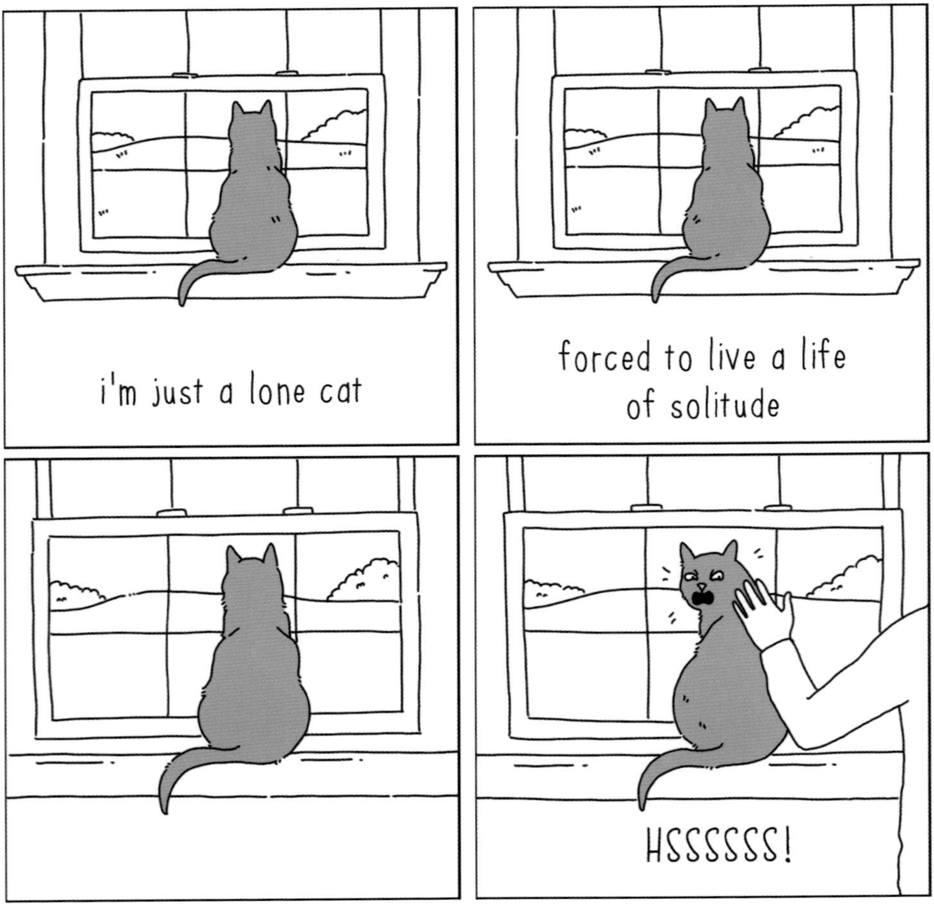
i'm just a lone cat
forced to live a life of solitude
HSSSSSS!

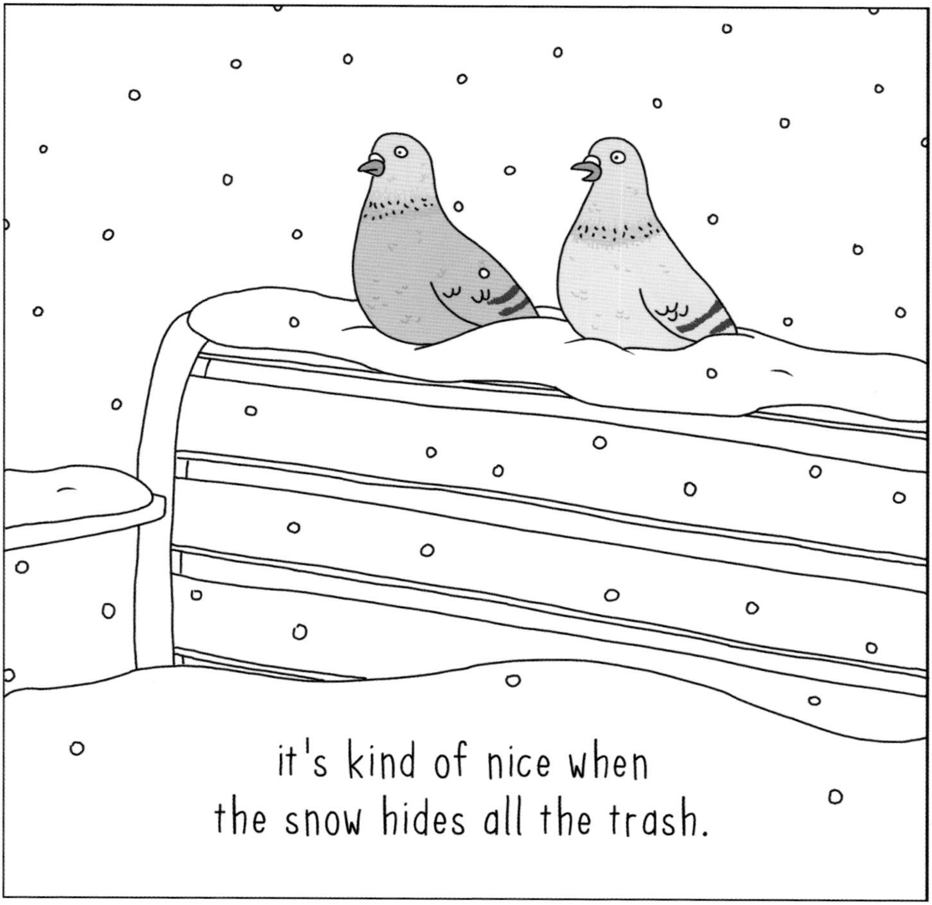
it's kind of nice when
the snow hides all the trash.

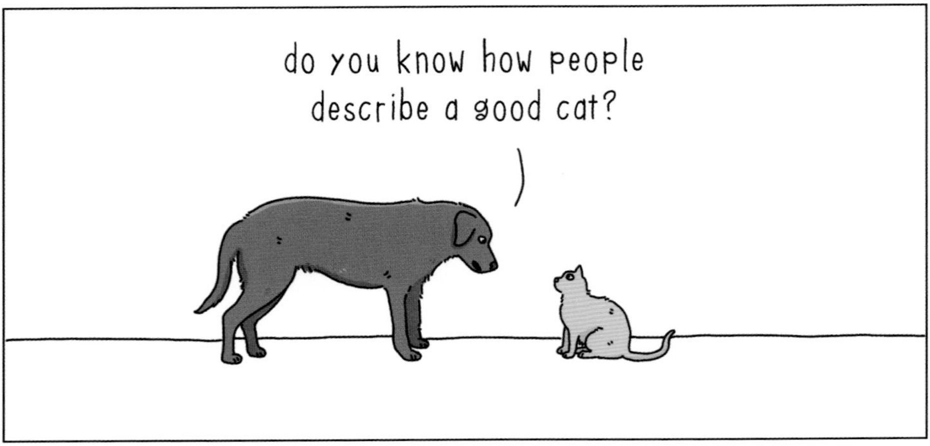
do you know how people
describe a good cat?

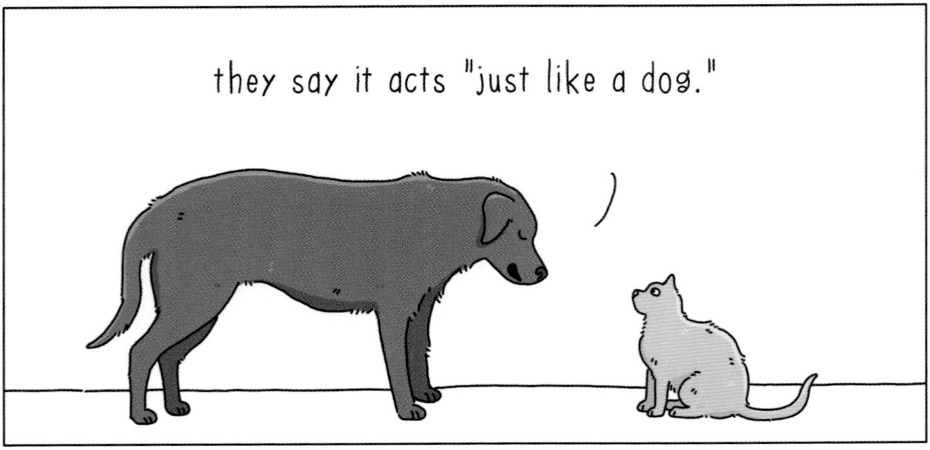
they say it acts "just like a dog."

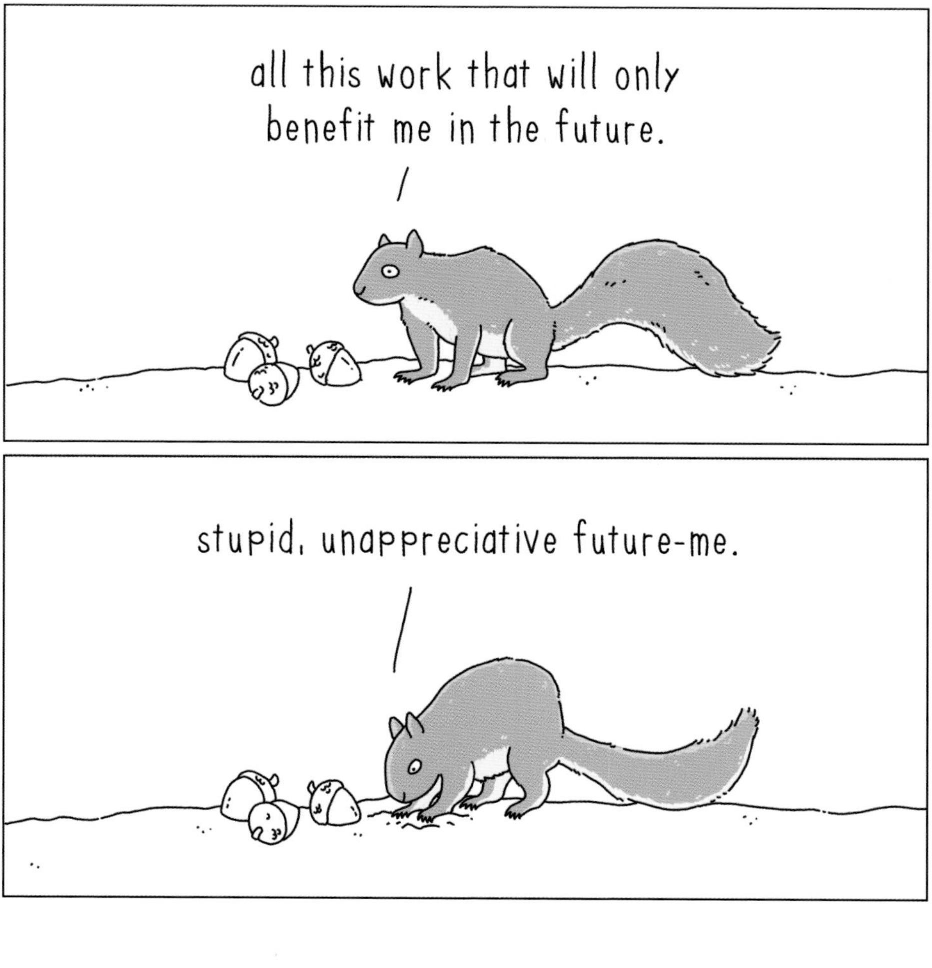
all this work that will only benefit me in the future.
stupid, unappreciative future-me.

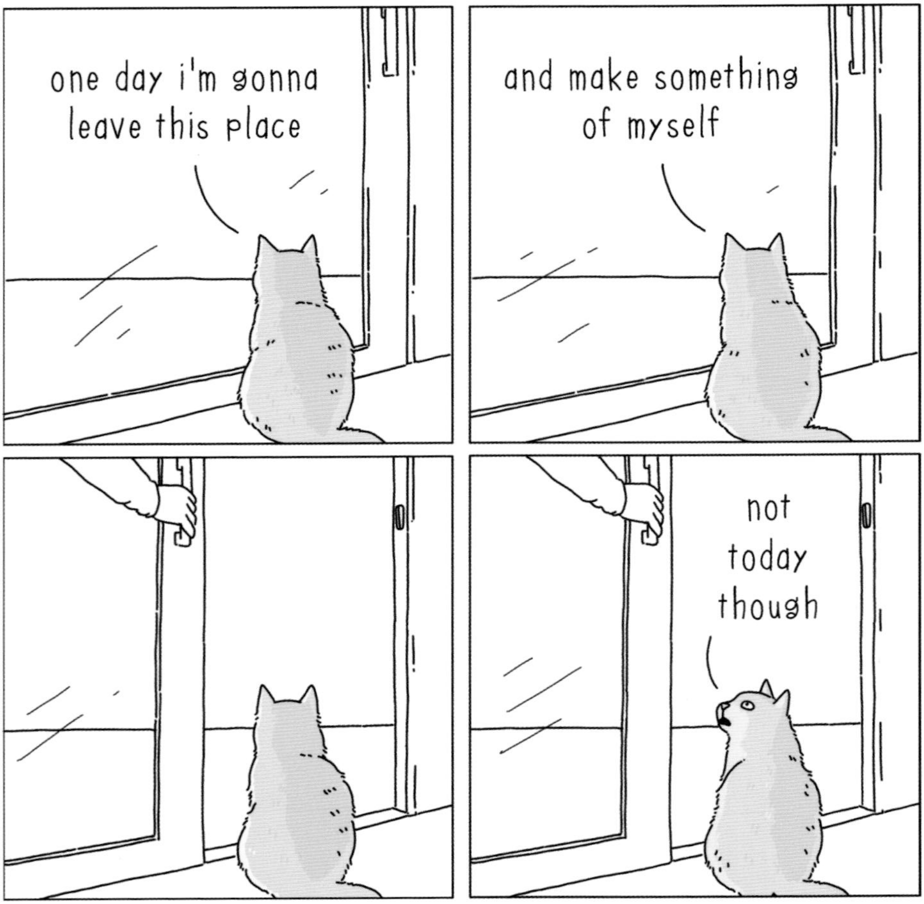
one day i'm gonna leave this place
and make something of myself
not today though

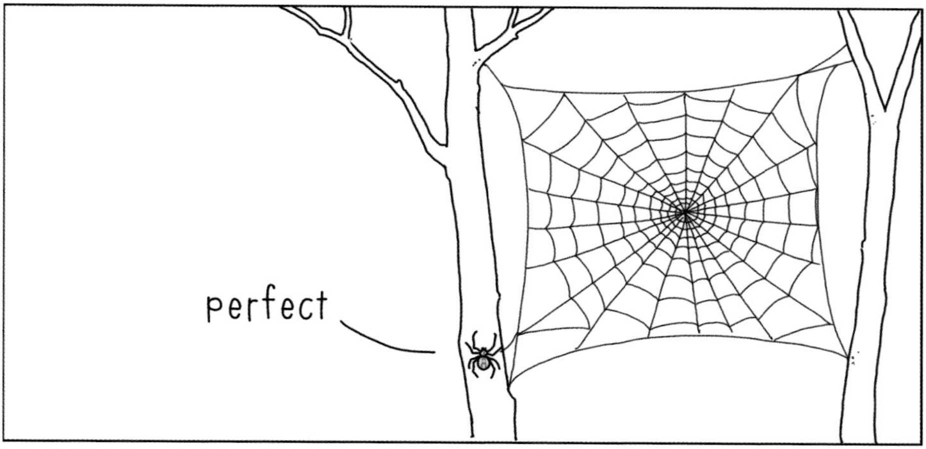
perfect

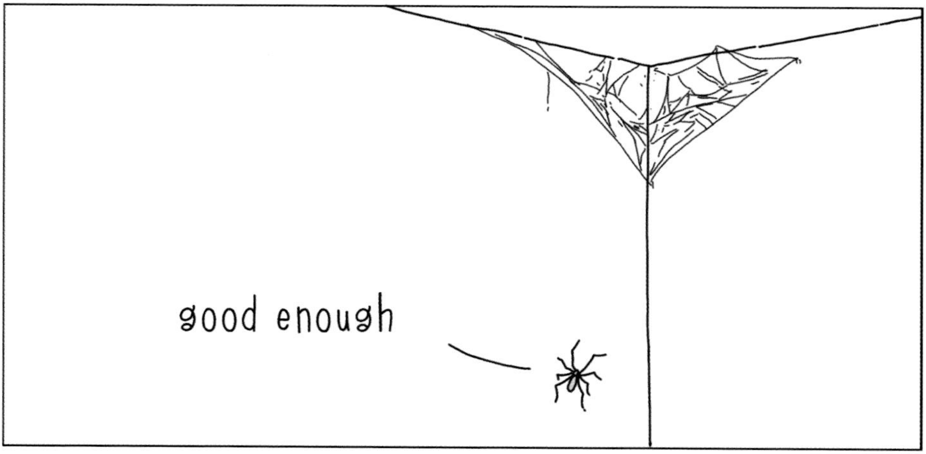
good enough

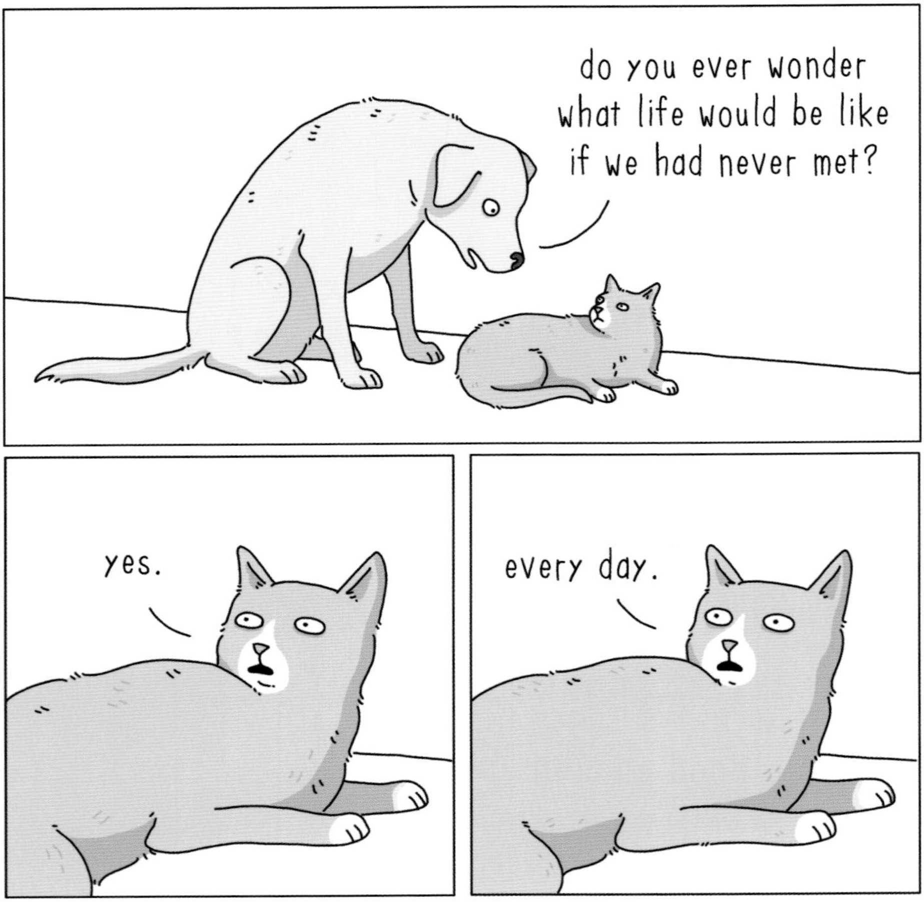
do you ever wonder what life would be like if we had never met?
yes.
every day.

about the author

Jimmy is a cartoonist and story artist from Massachusetts, where he lives with his wife, two kids, and two cats. He loves comics, animals, and short bios.